Adobe®
Photoshop® 6.0
Illustrated Introductory

Elizabeth Eisner Reding

COURSE
TECHNOLOGY
★
™
THOMSON LEARNING

Australia • Canada • Mexico • Singapore • Spain • United Kingdom • United States

COURSE TECHNOLOGY
™
THOMSON LEARNING

Adobe® Photoshop® 6.0—Illustrated Introductory
by Elizabeth Eisner Reding

Managing Editor
Nicole Jones Pinard

Product Manager
Rebecca Berardy

Associate Product Manager
Emeline Elliot

Production Editor
Kristen Guevara

Developmental Editor
Ann Fisher

Composition House
GEX Publishing Services

QA Manuscript Review
Jeff Schwartz, Ashlee Welz

Technical Reviewers
Sherry Bishop, Mike Nicholas

Text Designer
Joseph Lee,
Black Fish Design

Cover Designer
Doug Goodman,
Doug Goodman Designs

Exciting New Products

Try out Illustrated's New Product Line: Multimedia Tools

Multimedia tools teach students how to create text, graphics, video, animations, and sound, all of which can be incorporated for use in printed materials, Web pages, CD-ROMs, and multimedia presentations.

New Titles

▶ Adobe Photoshop 6.0—Illustrated Introductory (0-619-04595-7)

▶ Adobe Photoshop 5.5—Illustrated Introductory (0-7600-6337-0)

▶ Adobe Illustrator 9.0—Illustrated Introductory (0-619-01750-3)

▶ Macromedia Director 8 Shockwave Studio—Illustrated Introductory (0-619-01772-4)

▶ Macromedia Director 8 Shockwave Studio—Illustrated Complete (0-619-05658-4)

▶ Multimedia Concepts—Illustrated Introductory (0-619-01765-1)

▶ Macromedia Shockwave 8—Illustrated Essentials (0-619-05656-8)

▶ Macromedia Fireworks 4—Illustrated Essentials (0-619-05657-6)

Check Out Multimedia Concepts

Multimedia Concepts—Illustrated Introductory, by James E. Shuman, is the quick and visual way to learn cutting-edge multimedia concepts. This book studies the growth of multimedia, has an Internet focus in every unit, includes coverage of computer hardware requirements, and teaches students the principles of multimedia design. This eight-unit book has two hands-on units: Incorporating Multimedia into a Web site and Creating a Multimedia Application Using Macromedia® Director® 8.

A CD-ROM and companion Web site accompany this book and bring the concepts to life! This CD includes a time-limited trial version of Macromedia® Director® 8 to give students the tools they need to practice creating multimedia movies.

Enhance any Illustrated Text with these Exciting Products

Course Technology offers a continuum of solutions to meet your online learning needs. Three Distance Learning solutions enhance your classroom experience: MyCourse.com (hosted by Course Technology), Blackboard, and WebCT.

MyCourse.com is an easily customizable online syllabus and course enhancement tool. This tool adds value to your class by offering brand new content designed to reinforce what you are already teaching. MyCourse.com even allows you to add your own content, hyperlinks, and assignments.

WebCT and Blackboard are course management tools that deliver online content for eighty-five Course Technology titles. This growing list of titles enables instructors the ability to edit and add to any content made available through WebCT and Blackboard. In addition, you can choose what students access. The site is hosted on your school campus, allowing complete control over the information. WebCT and Blackboard offer their own internal communication system, including internal e-mail, Bulletin Boards, and Chat rooms. For more information please contact your Course Technology sales representative.

Create Your Ideal Course Package with CourseKits™

If one book doesn't offer all the coverage you need, create a course package that does. With Course Technology's CourseKits—our mix-and-match approach to selecting texts—you have the freedom to combine products from more than one series. When you choose any two or more Course Technology products for one course, we'll discount the price and package them together so your students can pick up one convenient bundle at the bookstore.

Preface

Welcome to *Adobe Photoshop 6.0—Illustrated Introductory.* This highly visual book offers users a hands-on introduction to Photoshop 6.0 and also serves as an excellent reference for future use.

This book is a member of Illustrated's Multimedia Tools series. These books teach students how to create text, graphics, video, animations, and sound for use in print publications, CD-ROM products, and Web-based applications. Check out books on Macromedia® Director® and Adobe® Illustrator® for more multimedia curriculum.

▶ Organization and Coverage

This text is organized into eight units with one appendix. In these units, students learn how to apply color techniques and add type to an image; use layers and channels; create special effects with filters; and make images ready for the Web with ImageReady 3.0. In addition, there is a helpful appendix, which covers using settings, preferences, and plug-ins to maximize Photoshop performance.

▶ About this Approach

What makes the Illustrated approach so effective at teaching software skills? It's quite simple. Each skill is presented on two facing pages, with the step-by-step instructions on the left page, and large screen illustrations on the right. Students can focus on a single skill without having to turn the page. This unique design makes information extremely accessible and easy to absorb, and provides a great reference for after the course is over. This hands-on approach also makes it ideal for both self-paced or instructor-led classes.

Each lesson, or "information display," contains the following elements:

Each 2-page spread focuses on a single skill.

Concise text that introduces the basic principles discussed in the lesson. Procedures are easier to learn when concepts fit into a framework.

Using the Layers Palette

Photoshop 6.0

Most Photoshop documents are composed of multiple layers. This layering process makes it easy to manipulate individual characteristics within a document by hiding and displaying different elements. The Layers palette displays all the layers within an open document. Using this palette, you can modify any layer, or control whether it is visible or not. The order in which the layers appear in the Layers palette matches the order in which they appear in the document. You can use the Layers palette to create, delete, merge, copy, or reposition layers. 🔊 Sharon wants to see how she can rearrange layers using the Layers palette.

Steps

QuickTip
You may see only the initial characters of the layer name due to the size of the window. You may need to resize the Layers palette to view all the layers.

1. Click the **Azaleas layer** in the Layers palette, as shown in Figure A-11
   Notice that the name of the highlighted active layer—in this case, Azaleas—appears in parentheses in the document title bar. The paintbrush icon that appears next to the thumbnail indicates that the layer can be modified.

2. Click the **eye button** on the **Azaleas layer** in the Layers palette
   The Azaleas layer is no longer visible, as shown in Figure A-11. The Show/Hide layer button is a toggle switch; you can redisplay the layer by clicking this button again. By default, transparent areas of an image have a checkerboard display in the Layers palette.

3. Click the **Show/Hide layer button** on the **Azaleas layer** in the Layers palette
   The Azaleas layer reappears in the document. You can also use the Layers palette to reposition a layer, which can affect the appearance of the document. Repositioning is accomplished by dragging a layer to a new position in the palette. You can move any layer up or down by one or more layers, depending on its initial location. You can also move it one layer at a time, move it to the front (top of the Layers palette), or to the back (bottom of the Layers palette). When you place the pointer over a layer, its appearance changes to .

QuickTip
Each time you close and reopen a file, the History palette is cleared.

4. Click the **Easter Lily layer** in the Layers palette, then drag it to the top position in the palette, as shown in Figure A-12
   As you drag the layer, the pointer changes to . The order of the layers in the palette changes, and part of the text appears *behind the white flower*, as shown in Figure A-13. Photoshop lets you modify your actions by offering 20 levels of undo. Each action you perform during a Photoshop session is recorded and made visible in the History palette.

5. Click **Layer Order** in the History palette, then drag it to the **Delete current state button** in the History palette, as shown in Figure A-13
   The Layer Order state is no longer visible in the History palette, the layers appear in their original order, and the image reverts to its original appearance.

6. Click **File** on the menu bar, then click **Save**
   It is a good idea to save your work early and often in the creation process, especially before making significant changes, or before printing.

CLUES TO USE

Using the History palette
Each task you complete on a Photoshop document is recorded in the History palette. This catalog of events makes it easy to see what changes occurred, and which tools or commands were used to make the modifications. Because only 20 states are retained in the History palette, the list of available changes you can make will constantly change. The oldest state in the History palette is at the top, while the most recent change is at the bottom of the list. Deleting a state in the History palette also erases all events that occurred *after* that state.

▶ PHOTOSHOP 12   **GETTING STARTED WITH ADOBE PHOTOSHOP 6.0**

QuickTips as well as troubleshooting advice right where you need it – next to the step itself.

Clear step-by-step directions, with what students are to type in green. When students follow the numbered steps, they quickly learn how each procedure is performed and what the results will be.

Clues to Use boxes provide concise information that either expands on one component of the major lesson skill or describes an independent task that is in some way related to the major lesson skill.

Every lesson features large-size, full-color representations of what the students' screen should look like after completing the numbered steps.

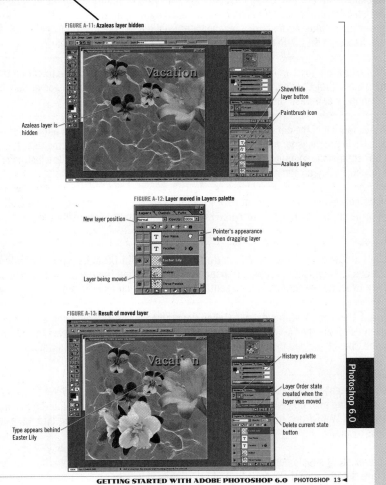

FIGURE A-11: Azaleas layer hidden

Azaleas layer is hidden

Show/Hide layer button

Paintbrush icon

Azaleas layer

FIGURE A-12: Layer moved in Layers palette

New layer position

Pointer's appearance when dragging layer

Layer being moved

FIGURE A-13: Result of moved layer

History palette

Layer Order state created when the layer was moved

Delete current state button

Type appears behind Easter Lily

Photoshop 6.0

GETTING STARTED WITH ADOBE PHOTOSHOP 6.0 PHOTOSHOP 13 ◄

Additional Features

The two-page lesson format featured in this book provides the new user with a powerful learning experience. Additionally, this book contains the following features:

► **Tryout Software**
At the back of this book, you will find a CD containing Tryout versions of Adobe® Photoshop 6.0® for both the Macintosh and Windows operating systems. Students can use this software to work through most of the exercises in this book. Note: The Tryout version does not enable you to save, export, or print artwork. For installation instruction, please see the Read This Before You Begin page.

► **Dual Platform**
The units in this book can be completed either on a Macintosh or on a Windows platform. The steps are written for both operating systems; however, the images throughout the book display the screens as they would appear in Windows.

► **Real-World Case**
The case study used throughout the textbook, a fictitious company called Zenith Design, is designed to be "real-world" in nature and introduces the kinds of activities that students will encounter when working with Photoshop. With a real-world case, the process of solving problems will be more meaningful to students.

► **End of Unit Material**
Each unit concludes with a Concepts Review that tests students' understanding of what they learned in the unit. The Concepts Review is followed by a Skills Review, which provides students with additional hands-on practice of the skills they learned in the unit. The Skills Review is followed by Independent Challenges, which pose case problems for students to solve. The Independent Challenges allow students to learn by exploring and to develop critical thinking skills. At least one Independent Challenge in each unit asks students to use the World Wide Web to solve the problem as indicated by an E-Quest icon. And one Independent Challenge in each unit encourages students to scan an image that will be used to complete the exercise. Visual Workshops that follow the Independent Challenges help students to develop critical thinking skills. Students are shown completed documents and are asked to recreate them from scratch.

V ◄

Instructor's Resource Kit

The Instructor's Resource Kit is Course Technology's way of putting the resources and information needed to teach and learn effectively into your hands. With an integrated array of teaching and learning tools that offers you and your students a broad range of technology-based instructional options, we believe this kit represents the highest quality and most cutting edge resources available to instructors today. Many of these resources are available at www.course.com. The resources available with this book are:

ExamView This textbook is accompanied by ExamView, a powerful testing software package that allows instructors to create and administer printed, computer (LAN-based), and Internet exams. ExamView includes hundreds of questions that correspond to the topics covered in this text, enabling students to generate detailed study guides that include page references for further review. The computer-based and Internet testing components allow students to take exams at their computers, and also save the instructor time by grading each exam automatically.

Instructor's Manual Available as an electronic file, the Instructor's Manual is quality-assurance tested and includes unit overviews, detailed lecture topics for each unit with teaching tips, an Upgrader's Guide, solutions to all lessons and end-of-unit material, and extra Independent Challenges. The Instructor's Manual is available on the Instructor's Resource Kit CD-ROM or you can download it from www.course.com.

Course Faculty Online Companion You can browse this textbook's password-protected site to obtain the Instructor's Manual, Solution Files, Project Files, and any updates to the text. Contact your Customer Service Representative for the site address and password.

Project Files Project Files contain all of the data that students will use to complete the lessons and end-of-unit material. A Readme file includes instructions for using the files. Adopters of this text are granted the right to install the Project Files on any standalone computer or network. The Project Files are available on the Instructor's Resource Kit CD-ROM, the Review Pack, and can also be downloaded from www.course.com.

Solution Files Solution Files contain every file students are asked to create or modify in the lessons and end-of-unit material. A Help file on the Instructor's Resource Kit includes information for using the Solution Files.

Figure Files The figures in the text are provided on the Instructor's Resource Kit CD to help you illustrate key topics or concepts. You can create traditional overhead transparencies by printing the figure files. Or you can create electronic slide shows by using the figures in a presentation program such as PowerPoint.

Student Online Companion This book features its own Online Companion where students can go to access Web sites that will help them complete the Webwork Independent Challenges. Because the Web is constantly changing, the Student Online Companion will provide the reader with current updates regarding links referenced in the book.

WebCT WebCT is a tool used to create Web-based educational environments and also uses WWW browsers as the interface for the course-building environment. The site is hosted on your school campus, allowing complete control over the information. WebCT has its own internal communication system, offering internal e-mail, a Bulletin Board, and a Chat room.

Course Technology offers pre-existing supplemental information to help in your WebCT class creation, such as a suggested Syllabus, Lecture Notes, Student Downloads, and Test Banks in which you can schedule an exam, create reports, and more.

Brief Contents

Contents

Photoshop 6.0

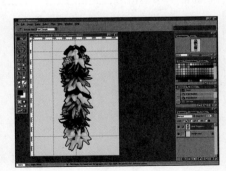

Contents

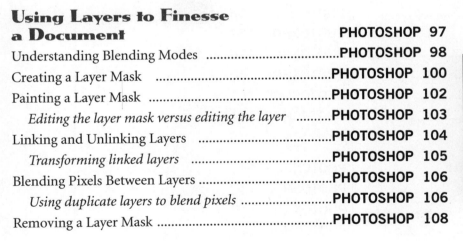

Contents

Creating Web Documents   PHOTOSHOP 169

Contents

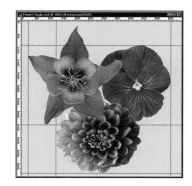

Read This Before You Begin

Project Files

To complete the lessons and end-of-unit material in this book, students need to obtain the necessary project files. Please refer to the instructions on the front inside cover for various methods of getting these files. Once obtained, the user selects where to store the files, such as to the hard disk drive, network server, or Zip disk.

Free Tryout Software

Included on a CD with this book is the Adobe Photoshop 6.0 Tryout software. This same software is available as a free download from the Adobe Corporation Web site (*http://www.adobe.com*).

Installation instructions for the included CD-ROM are as follows:

- **Windows**: Insert the CD in the CD-ROM drive, open Windows Explorer, select the CD-ROM drive, double-click the Setup file in the Photoshop 6.0 Tryout folder, then follow the on-screen instructions to complete the installation.

- **Macintosh**: Insert the CD in the CD-ROM drive, double-click the CD icon, double-click the Adobe Photoshop Tryout icon, then follow the on-screen instructions to complete the installation.

If you are using the Adobe Photoshop 6.0 Tryout software, you cannot save, print, export, drag and drop, use the Clipboard, or use all of the filter capabilities. To print screen results, students can use Print Screen, and then copy or move the image into any graphics capable program.

To Use Print Screen:

- **Windows**: Click [Print Screen], open a graphics capable program such as Microsoft Paint, click Edit on the menu bar, and click Paste to paste the screen into Paint.

- **Macintosh**: Press and hold [Shift] [Command] [3] to create a graphics file on the hard disk drive, and then open the file in a graphics capable program.

Getting
Started with Adobe Photoshop 6.0

Objectives

► **Define digital imaging software**
► **Start Adobe Photoshop 6.0**
► **View the Photoshop window**
► **Open and save a document**
► **Get Help**
► **Use the Layers palette**
► **View and print a document**
► **Close a document and exit Photoshop**

Adobe Photoshop is an image-editing program that lets you create original artwork, manipulate color images, and retouch photographs. In addition to being a robust application popular with graphics professionals, it is practical for anyone who wants to enhance existing artwork or create new masterpieces. In this unit, you will learn how to start Photoshop and use menus and elements found in the Photoshop window. You will also learn how to open and save an existing file, use the extensive Help system, use the Layers palette, and view and print a Photoshop document. ✎ Sharon Mezoff is an intern at Zenith Design, a small advertising agency. During her internship, Sharon will work on a variety of graphics projects. Acquainting herself with Photoshop is one of her first priorities.

Photoshop 6.0

Defining Digital Imaging Software

Photoshop is an image-editing program. An **image-editing** program lets you manipulate graphic images that can be reproduced by professional printers using full-color processes. Using palettes, tools, and a variety of techniques, you can modify a Photoshop document by rotating it, resizing it, changing its colors, or adding text. Photoshop files have the .PSD extension added to their file-names, but they can also be saved as other types of commonly used file formats. Table A-1 lists these file formats as well as formats that Photoshop can open. As an intern, Sharon will need to use Photoshop to complete various projects. Many companies use Photoshop because of its broad capabilities, which are described below.

Details

QuickTip

Photoshop files can become quite large. Once complete, a file can be *flattened*, a process that combines all layers and reduces the file size.

QuickTip

You can use external devices, such as a *scanner* or *digital camera*, to create your own electronic image files, and then manipulate them in Photoshop.

QuickTip

Actions are recorded for the current session only, and are discarded when Photoshop closes.

Use layers
Each Photoshop document can be made up of one layer or many individual layers. A **layer** is a section within a document that can be manipulated independently. All the layers in a document are equivalent to individual clear sheets of paper that form a stack. Each layer can be modified using the tools in Photoshop. Layers allow you to control individual elements within a document, and create great dramatic effects, such as an image fading into the background. Figure A-1 shows a document with multiple layers, including type, water, and flowers. You can create different effects and variations of the same document by hiding specific layers. Imagine how different this document would look if you hid the Easter Lily or Azaleas layers.

Manipulate images
Using the Lasso Tool, you can outline sections of one layer and drag them onto another layer. Within a document, you can add new items, modify existing elements, change colors, and draw shapes.

Design logos
A **logo** is a distinctive icon created by combining symbols, shapes, colors, and text. Logos are used to give graphic identity to organizations, such as corporations, universities, and retail stores.

Create and format text
You can create and format text, called **type** in Photoshop. A variety of special effects, including the ability to control the distance between characters, can be applied to type. You can also edit type after it is created and formatted.

Undo and redo tasks using the History palette
Each change you make to a Photoshop document is recorded in the History palette. Recorded actions can be undone and redone, as necessary.

Extract objects
You may want to copy a specific area of one layer onto another layer, or isolate a foreground or background image. Even if an image has a complex set of edges, you can extract portions of it and use it elsewhere.

Integrate with Adobe ImageReady
Adobe ImageReady is a program that allows you to optimize, preview, and animate images for use on Web pages. Because ImageReady is fully integrated with Photoshop, you can jump seamlessly between the two programs.

Produce Web-ready graphics
You can quickly turn graphic images into GIF animations. Photoshop and ImageReady let you compress file size while optimizing image quality to ensure fast download times from Web pages. Using special optimization features, you can view multiple versions of a document and select the one you want.

FIGURE A-1: Sample document

TABLE A-1: Common graphic file formats

file format	filename extension	file format	filename extension
Bitmap	.BMP	Filmstrip	.VLM
PC Paintbrush	.PCX	Kodak PhotoCD	.PCD
Graphics Interchange Format	.GIF	Pixar	.PXR
Photoshop PostScript	.EPS	Scitex CT	.SCT
Tagged Image Format	.TIF	Photoshop PDF	.PDF
JPEG Picture Format	.JPG or .JPE	Targa	.TGA or .VDA
CorelDraw	.CDR	PICT file	.PCT or .PIC

Photoshop 6.0

Starting Adobe Photoshop 6.0

There are different ways to start Photoshop depending on the type of computer you are using. When you start Photoshop, the computer displays a splash screen—a window that displays information about the software, and then the Photoshop window opens. ✎ Photoshop is the image-editing program of choice for Zenith Design, and it is used on both Windows and Macintosh computers throughout the company. Sharon starts Photoshop to begin her work.

WIN

1. Click the **Start button** 🔲Start on the taskbar

The Start button is on the left side of the taskbar and is used to start programs on your computer.

Trouble?

The Adobe Photoshop 6.0 program is in the Adobe folder, which is in the Program Files folder on the hard drive.

2. Point to **Programs**, point to the **Adobe folder**, point to the **Photoshop 6.0 folder**, if necessary, then click the **Adobe Photoshop 6.0 program icon** 🖼

The Programs menu lists all the programs, including Adobe Photoshop, that are installed on your computer, as shown in Figure A-2. Your Programs menu might look different depending on the programs you have installed. When Photoshop opens, the work area appears.

3. Click **File** on the menu bar, then click **New**

The New dialog box opens. You can use this dialog box to give the file a meaningful name and determine the document size.

4. Click **OK**

A new blank window appears.

MAC

1. Double-click the **hard drive icon** as shown in Figure A-3, then double-click the **Adobe Photoshop 6.0 folder**

If you do not see the Adobe Photoshop 6.0 folder see your instructor or technical support person for assistance.

2. Double-click the **Adobe Photoshop 6.0 program icon** 🖼

Photoshop opens, displaying the work area.

3. Click **File** on the menu bar, then click **New**

The New dialog box opens. You can use this dialog box to give the file a meaningful name and determine the document size.

QuickTip

Desktop items are visible when Photoshop is open.

4. Click **OK**

A new blank window appears.

FIGURE A-2: Starting Photoshop 6.0 (Windows)

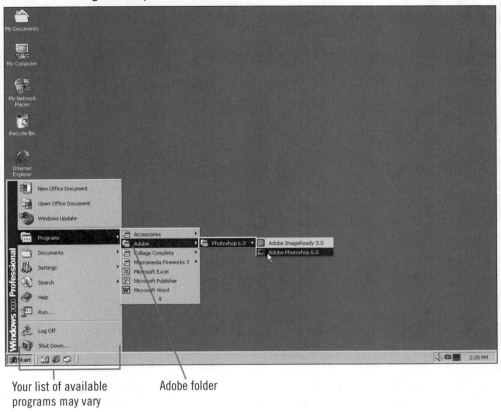

Your list of available programs may vary

Adobe folder

FIGURE A-3: Starting Photoshop 6.0 (Macintosh)

Macintosh hard drive icon

Photoshop 6.0

Photoshop 6.0

Viewing the Photoshop Window

The **work area** is the space within the program window where a new or existing document appears and is edited. The work area also contains the toolbox and palettes. **Palettes** are small windows within the work area that let you edit and add effects to a document. As you use tools, the appearance of the Photoshop window changes. You can return the tools to their default settings by clicking Edit on the menu bar, pointing to Preferences, clicking General, clicking Reset All Tools, then clicking OK. ━━━ Sharon takes time to familiarize herself with the elements of the Photoshop work area. Refer to the descriptions below and locate these elements in Figure A-4.

 Details

 The **title bar** displays the program name (Adobe Photoshop) and the filename of the open document (in this case, **Untitled-1** because the file has not been named). The title bar also contains the Close, Minimize, Maximize, and Restore buttons.

 The **menu bar** contains menus of Photoshop commands. You can choose a menu command by clicking it, pressing [Alt] plus the underlined letter in the menu name (Win). Some commands display shortcut keys on the right side of the menu. Shortcut keys provide an alternate way to activate menu commands. Some commands may appear dimmed, which means they are not currently available. Commands with an ellipsis indicate additional choices.

 The **toolbox** contains tools associated with frequently used Photoshop commands. The face of a tool contains a graphic representation of its function; for example, the Zoom Tool has a magnifying glass on its face. Place the pointer over each tool to display a ScreenTip, which tells you the name or function of that tool. Some tools are hidden from view, indicated by a small black triangle in the lower-right corner of the tool.

 The **tool options bar**, located directly under the menu bar, displays the current settings for each tool. For example, when you click the Type Tool, the default font and font size appear in the tool options bar and can be changed if desired. The tool options bar can be moved anywhere in the work area for easier access.

 Palettes are small windows used to verify settings and modify documents. The appearance of a palette depends on which tool is active. By default, palettes appear in stacked groups at the right side of the window, but they can be separated from the groups and moved anywhere in the work area by dragging the palette's name tab. Each palette contains a menu that you can view by clicking the list arrow in its upper-right corner.

 The **status bar** is located at the bottom of the program window (Win) or the document window (Mac). It displays information, such as the file size of the active window, and a description of the active tool. You can display other information, such as the current tool, by clicking the black triangle on the status bar to view a pull down menu with more options.

 The **work area** includes the entire window, from the menu bar to the status bar (Win). Desktop items are visible in this area (Mac).

Rulers can help you precisely measure and position an object in the work area. The rulers do not appear the first time you use Photoshop, but they can be displayed using the View menu.

FIGURE A-4: Photoshop window

Tool options bar

Work area

Navigator palette

Color palette

History palette

Layers palette

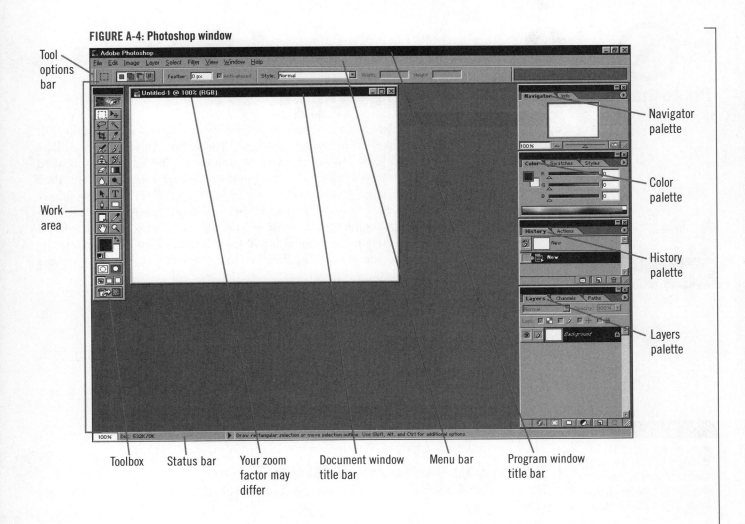

Toolbox   Status bar   Your zoom factor may differ   Document window title bar   Menu bar   Program window title bar

Opening and Saving a Document

Photoshop 6.0

Sometimes it's more efficient to create a new image by modifying an existing one, especially if it contains layers and special effects that you want to use again. Throughout this book, you will be instructed to open your Project Files and use the Save As command. The **Save As** command creates a copy of the file, and prompts you to give the duplicate file a new name. You will then modify the new file, by following the lesson steps. Saving your Project Files with new names keeps them intact in case you have to start the lesson over again, or you wish to repeat an exercise. ✎ Sharon's first assignment is to revise an advertising campaign file started by a previous intern. She is asked to retain the original file so that Zenith's client can compare the new file to the old one. Sharon opens the existing file, then uses the Save As command to create a copy of the file with a new name.

1. Click **File** on the menu bar, then click **Open**
The Open dialog box opens.

2. Click the **Look in list arrow (Win)** or the **Current file location list arrow (Mac)**, then click the **drive and folder where your Project Files are stored**
A list of the Project Files appears. Figure A-5 shows the list of files in Windows, and Figure A-6 shows the list of files in Macintosh.

Macintosh

If you receive a message stating that some text layers need to be updated before they can be used for vector-based output, click Update.

3. Click **PS A-1**, then click **Open**
The file opens. Notice that the filename appears in the document's title bar.

4. Click **File** on the menu bar, then click **Save As**
The Save As dialog box opens. You use the Save As command to create a copy of this file with a new filename.

5. If the drive containing your Project Files does not appear, click the **Save in list arrow (Win)** or the **Current file location list arrow (Mac)**, then click the **drive and folder that contains your Project Files**

6. Select the current filename in the File name text box, if necessary, type **Vacation**, then click **Save**
The Save As dialog box closes, the file PS A-1 closes, and a duplicate file named Vacation is now open, as shown in Figure A-7. Notice that the existing blank window is still open, but hidden behind the new document. To save future changes as you continue to work, you can click File on the menu bar, then click Save.

Using Save As versus Save

The Save As command is used to name an unnamed document, or to save an existing file with a new name. This command lets you create a duplicate file that you can then modify, while the existing file is unchanged. The Save command is used to keep modifications you made to an existing file. For example, you could use the Save command to preserve recent changes *prior* to trying a new technique. If the new changes don't work, you can close the file *without* saving the changes.

FIGURE A-5: Open dialog box (Win)

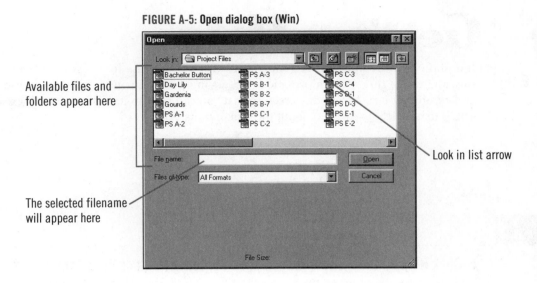

Available files and folders appear here

Look in list arrow

The selected filename will appear here

FIGURE A-6: Open dialog box (Mac)

Current file location list arrow

Available files and folders appear here

FIGURE A-7: Vacation document

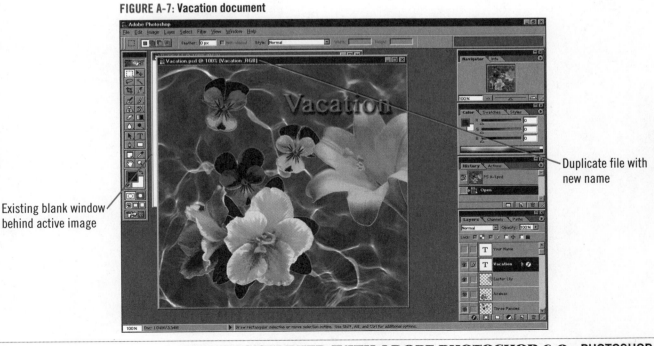

Existing blank window behind active image

Duplicate file with new name

Photoshop 6.0

Getting Help

Photoshop features an extensive Help system that you can use to access definitions, explanations, and useful tips. Help information appears in a browser window. You can resize the Help window, and set it to appear on-screen so that you can refer to it as you work. ✐ Sharon decides to use Help to find out about the tool options bar.

1. Click **Help** on the menu bar, then click **Contents (Win)** or **Help Contents (Mac)**
   Your browser window opens, as shown in Figure A-8. You can select a topic listed on the left side of the screen. You can also open the Help window by pressing **[F1]** (Win).

Trouble?

If necessary, resize the window.

2. Click **Looking at the Work Area**
   The Looking at the Work Area window appears, as shown in Figure A-9.

QuickTip

Print a Help topic by clicking the Print button on the browser toolbar.

3. Click **Using the tool options bar**
   Information about the tool options bar appears, as shown in Figure A-10. The two arrow buttons on the Help window let you move forward and backward through any windows opened during the current Help session.

4. Click **File** on the menu bar, then click **Close (Win)** or **Quit (Mac)** when you finish reading

FIGURE A-8: Initial Photoshop 6.0 Help window

Index

List of available topics

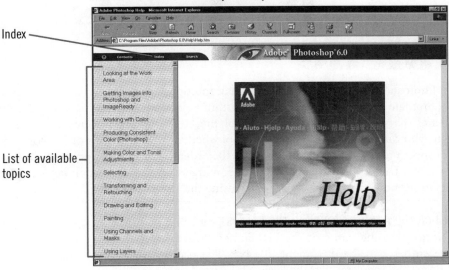

FIGURE A-9: Topic choices

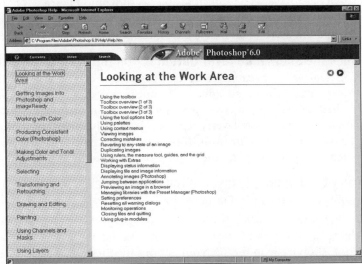

FIGURE A-10: Tool options bar information

Help window navigation buttons

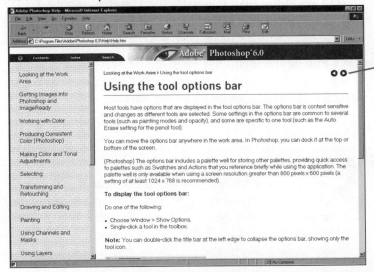

Photoshop 6.0

Using the Layers Palette

Most Photoshop documents are composed of multiple layers. This layering process makes it easy to manipulate individual characteristics within a document by hiding and displaying different elements. The **Layers palette** displays all the layers within an open document. Using this palette, you can modify any layer, or control whether it is visible or not. The order in which the layers appear in the Layers palette matches the order in which they appear in the document. You can use the Layers palette to create, delete, merge, copy, or reposition layers. Sharon wants to see how she can rearrange layers using the Layers palette.

Steps

QuickTip

You may see only the initial characters of the layer name due to the size of the window. You may need to resize the Layers palette to view all the layers.

1. Click the **Azaleas layer** in the Layers palette, as shown in Figure A-11

Notice that the name of the highlighted **active layer**—in this case, Azaleas—appears in parentheses in the document title bar. The paintbrush icon that appears next to the thumbnail indicates that the layer can be modified.

2. Click the **eye button** on the **Azaleas layer** in the Layers palette

The Azaleas layer is no longer visible, as shown in Figure A-11. The Show/Hide layer button is a toggle switch; you can redisplay the layer by clicking this button again. By default, transparent areas of an image have a checkerboard display in the Layers palette.

3. Click the **Show/Hide layer button** on the **Azaleas layer** in the Layers palette

The Azaleas layer reappears in the document. You can also use the Layers palette to reposition a layer, which can affect the appearance of the document. Repositioning is accomplished by dragging a layer to a new position in the palette. You can move any layer up or down by one or more layers, depending on its initial location. You can also move it one layer at a time, move it to the front (top of the Layers palette), or to the back (bottom of the Layers palette). When you place the pointer over a layer, its appearance changes to.

QuickTip

Each time you close and reopen a file, the History palette is cleared.

4. Click the **Easter Lily layer** in the Layers palette, then drag it to the top position in the palette, as shown in Figure A-12

As you drag the layer, the pointer changes to. The order of the layers in the palette changes, and part of the text appears *behind the white flower*, as shown in Figure A-13. Photoshop lets you modify your actions by offering 20 levels of undo. Each action you perform during a Photoshop session is recorded and made visible in the **History palette**.

5. Click **Layer Order** in the History palette, then drag it to the **Delete current state button** in the History palette, as shown in Figure A-13

The Layer Order state is no longer visible in the History palette, the layers appear in their original order, and the image reverts to its original appearance.

6. Click **File** on the menu bar, then click **Save**

It is a good idea to save your work early and often in the creation process, especially before making significant changes, or before printing.

Using the History palette

Each task you complete on a Photoshop document is recorded in the History palette. This catalog of events makes it easy to see what changes occurred, and which tools or commands were used to make the modifications. Because only 20 states are retained in the History palette, the list of available changes you can make will constantly change. The oldest state in the History palette is at the top, while the most recent change is at the bottom of the list. Deleting a state in the History palette also erases all events that occurred *after* that state.

FIGURE A-11: Azaleas layer hidden

Azaleas layer is
hidden

Show/Hide
layer button

Paintbrush icon

Azaleas layer

FIGURE A-12: Layer moved in Layers palette

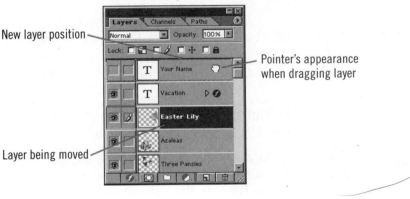

New layer position

Layer being moved

Pointer's appearance
when dragging layer

FIGURE A-13: Result of moved layer

Type appears behind
Easter Lily

History palette

Layer Order state
created when the
layer was moved

Delete current state
button

Photoshop 6.0

Viewing and Printing a Document

Photoshop 6.0

In many cases, a professional print shop may be the best option for printing a Photoshop document with the highest quality. You can, however, print a Photoshop document using a standard black-and-white or color printer. Regardless of the number of layers in a document, your printout will be a composite of all visible layers. Of course, the quality of your printer will affect the appearance of your output. Table A-2 provides basic printing tips that may be helpful. Before printing, you can use the Zoom Tool to enlarge or reduce your view. Zooming in or out enlarges or reduces your viewpoint, not the actual image. ✎ Sharon is asked to print the Vacation document, but first she wants to practice using the Zoom Tool.

Trouble?

If a file is sent to print and the printer is turned off or is offline, an error message may appear.

1. Make sure the printer is on and contains paper

2. Click the **Zoom Tool** 🔍 on the toolbox, the pointer changes to ⊕
The tool options bar changes its appearance to display options for enlarging or reducing the size of the image.

3. Click the **Resize Windows To Fit checkbox** on the tool options bar ▣
The document window—the frame surrounding the image—will also be resized as the image is magnified or reduced.

QuickTip

Zooming out is like *stepping back*: The scale gets smaller and you can see more of the image. Zooming in is like *stepping forward*: You see less of an image, but in larger, greater detail.

4. Press **[Alt] (Win)** or **[Option] (Mac)**, the pointer changes to ⊖, then click the **center** of the image
The area is reduced, as shown in Figure A-14. You can zoom out more by clicking the image again, or you can zoom in again.

5. Release **[Alt] (Win)** or **[Option] (Mac)**, then click ⊕ in the **center** of the image
The image returns to its original magnification.

Macintosh

If you did not select a printer using the Chooser, a warning box may appear.

6. Click **File** on the menu bar, then click **Page Setup**
The Page Setup dialog box, as shown in Figure A-15, opens, displaying options for printing, such as orientation. **Orientation** is the direction an image appears on the page. In **Portrait orientation**, a document is printed with the short edge of the paper at the top and bottom. In **Landscape orientation**, a document is printed with the long edge of the paper at the top and bottom.

7. Click the **Landscape option button**, then click **OK**
Now you are ready to print.

QuickTip

If necessary to distinguish your work, double-click the type layer thumbnail **T** on the Your Name layer in the Layers palette, type your name, then click the Move Tool ⊕.

8. Click **File** on the menu bar, click **Print**, then click **Proceed**
The Print dialog box opens, as shown in Figure A-16.

9. Make sure that the **All option button** is selected, and that **1** appears in the **Copies text box**, then click **OK (Win)** or **Print (Mac)**
Review the document to see if it printed as you expected.

TABLE A-2: Image printing tips

before you print	recommendation
Check the printer	Make sure that the printer is turned on, is online, and has paper. Make sure the color cartridges, if any, are clean, and there are no error messages or warning signals.
Check the printer selection	Use the Printer Name command in the Print dialog box to make sure the correct printer is selected.

FIGURE A-14: Reduced image

Tool options bar changes

Zoom Tool

Your zoom factor may differ

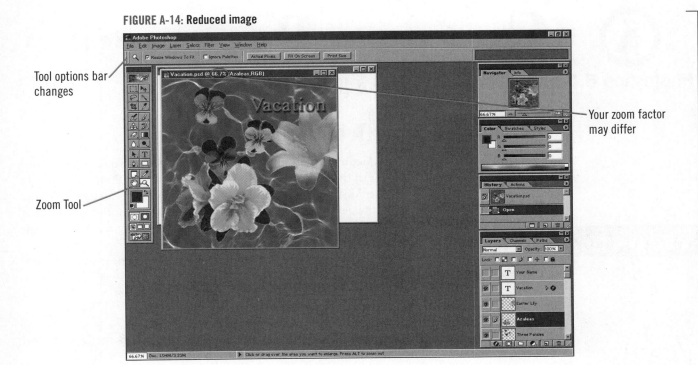

FIGURE A-15: Page Setup dialog box

Name list arrow

Your printer may be different

Orientation options

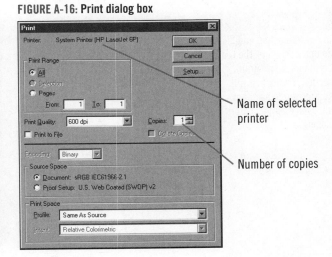

FIGURE A-16: Print dialog box

Name of selected printer

Number of copies

CLUES TO USE

Using a scanner and a digital camera

In addition to using a scanner to create electronic files, you can import photographs to your computer in digital form, using a digital camera. If you have a scanner, you can use print images, such as those taken from photographs, magazines, or line drawings, in Photoshop. Scanners are relatively inexpensive and simple to use. They come in many types, including flatbed or single-sheet feed. Once an image is scanned and saved as an electronic file, you can open and use it in Photoshop. See your instructor to learn how to use the scanner in your facility. You can also use a digital camera to create your own images. Although it operates much like a film camera, a digital camera does not contain film. Instead, it contains some form of electronic media, such as a floppy disk or SmartMedia card, onto which it captures images. Once you upload the images from your camera to your computer, you can use them in Photoshop.

Photoshop 6.0

Closing a Document and Exiting Photoshop

When you finish working on a document, you must save and close it. When you complete your work in Photoshop, you should exit the program. Closing a document leaves Photoshop open so you can open or create another document. Exiting Photoshop closes the document, closes Photoshop, and returns you to the desktop, where you can choose to open another program or shut down the computer. Sharon is unexpectedly called to a meeting, so she closes the document, and then exits Photoshop.

Steps

1. Click **File** on the menu bar

The File menu opens, as shown in Figure A-17.

2. Click **Close**

The Vacation file closes, leaving the blank document open. You can also click the Close button on the title bar to close the file.

3. If asked to save your work, click **Yes (Win)** or **Save (Mac)**

Photoshop closes the file and displays the blank, untitled document.

4. Click **File** on the menu bar, then click **Exit (Win)** or **Quit (Mac)**

You can also double-click the program control menu box (Win) to exit the program. Photoshop closes, which frees up substantial computer memory for other tasks.

QuickTip

To exit Photoshop and close an open file, click the Close button in the program window. Photoshop will prompt you to save any unsaved changes before closing.

FIGURE A-17: Closing a document using the File menu

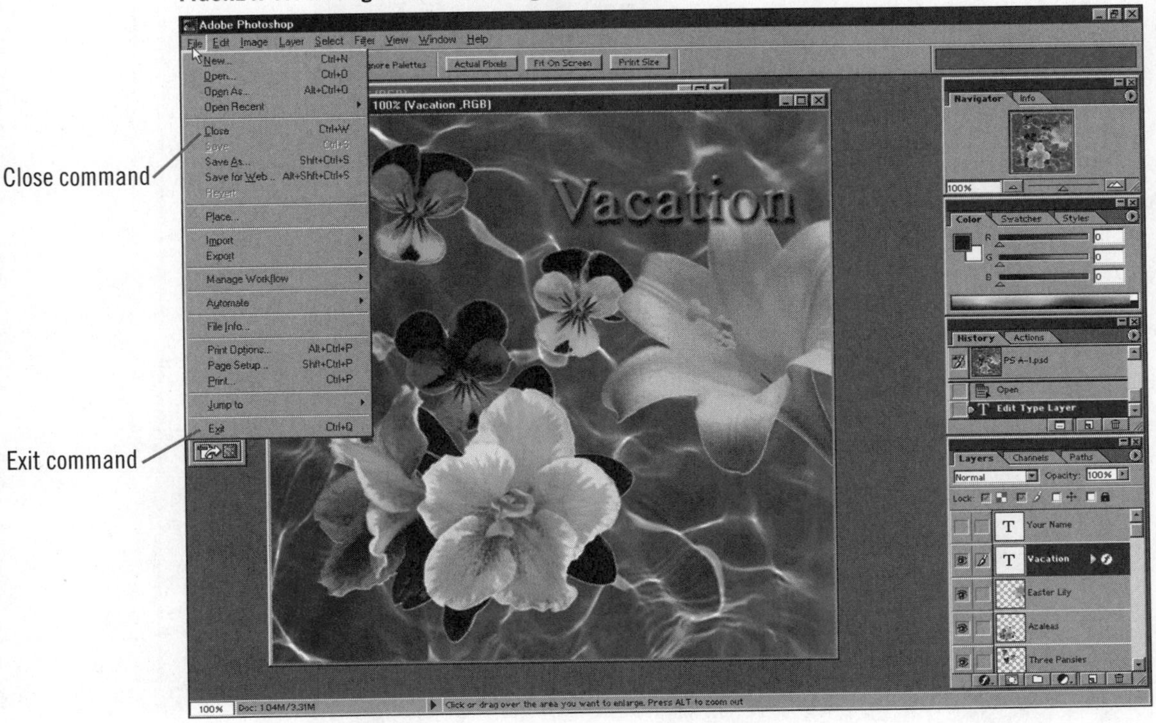

Close command →

Exit command →

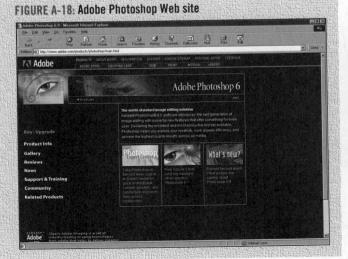

CLUES TO USE

Using Adobe Photoshop's Web site

You can get more information about Photoshop on the Adobe Photoshop Web site, which offers tips and how-to information, as well as new product developments and special offers. The URL for the Adobe Photoshop Web site is *http://www.adobe.com*. By clicking the hyperlinks provided, you will find additional information on Photoshop and other Adobe products. Figure A-18 shows the Adobe Photoshop home page. Because this site is updated often, your screen may look different. To find additional sites on the Internet with Photoshop information, you can use your favorite search engine, as well as the links found within the Adobe Photoshop site.

FIGURE A-18: Adobe Photoshop Web site

Photoshop 6.0

Practice

► Concepts Review

Label each element in the Photoshop window shown in Figure A-19.

FIGURE A-19

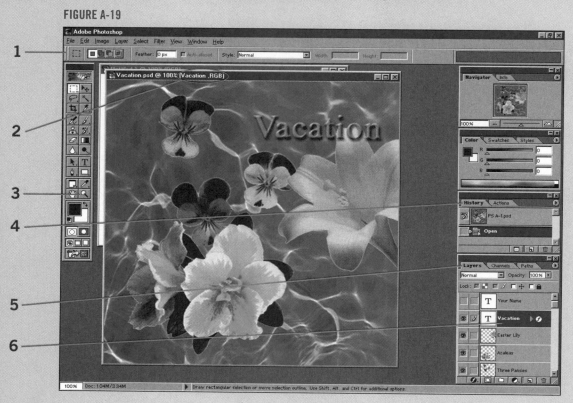

Match each button, tool, or pointer with the statement that describes its function.

7. Show/Hide layer button
8. Zoom in pointer
9. Dragging pointer
10. Zoom out pointer
11. Deletes current layer
12. Layer can be modified

a.
b.
c.
d.
e.
f.

Select the best answer from the list of choices.

13. **Where does the name of the active layer appear?**
    a. Document window title bar
    b. Program window title bar
    c. Status bar
    d. Taskbar

14. **Which feature in the work area contains settings for the active tool?**
    a. Tool Specific bar
    b. Tool Toolbox bar
    c. Menu bar
    d. None of the above

15. **Which tool is used to zoom in on a selected area?**
    a.
    b.
    c.
    d.

16. **Which key is pressed while using the Zoom Tool to zoom out of an area?**
    a. [Shift]
    b. [Ctrl] (Win) or [Command] (Mac)
    c. [Alt] (Win) or [Option] (Mac)
    d. [Enter] (Win) or [Return] (Mac)

17. **Which information is obtained from the History palette?**
    a. Previous dates the file was modified
    b. Last five actions
    c. Number of modifications made in the previous session
    d. Last 20 actions

18. **The area containing open images and palettes is called the**
    a. Work spot.
    b. Work area.
    c. Workplace.
    d. Workbench.

19. **The area containing commonly used tools is called the**
    a. Tool kit.
    b. Tool bench.
    c. Toolbox.
    d. Tool case.

Photoshop 6.0

20. **Which menu is used to exit Photoshop?**
    a. File
    b. Image
    c. Select
    d. Window

21. **Which command is used to save an existing file with another name?**
    a. Save Additional
    b. Save
    c. Save As
    d. Save Other

22. **Which program is used to optimize images?**
    a. Photoshop only
    b. ImageReady only
    c. Both Photoshop and ImageReady
    d. Neither Photoshop nor ImageReady

23. **Which button indicates that a layer can be modified?**
    a.
    b.
    c.
    d.

24. **Which statement about the status bar is *incorrect*?**
    a. It can display document sizes.
    b. It is located in a floating palette.
    c. It can be modified.
    d. It displays a description of the active tool.

25. **Which pointer appears when you drag a layer?**
    a.
    b.
    c.
    d.

▶ Skills Review

1. **Start Adobe Photoshop 6.0.**
   a. Start Photoshop.
   b. Create a new document that is 500 pixels wide by 500 pixels high, and name the new document *Review*.
   c. Locate the area containing the document name.
   d. Locate the menu that is used to open a new document.
   e. View the toolbox, the tool options bar, and the palettes that are showing.
   f. Click the Zoom Tool, then view the change in the tool options bar.

2. Open and save a document.
   a. Open PS A-2 from the drive and folder where your Project Files are stored.
   b. Save the publication as *Zenith Design Logo*.

3. Get Help.
   a. Open the Adobe Photoshop 6.0 Help Contents window.
   b. Using the Contents panel, find information on using layers.
   c. Find information about using the Layers palette.
   d. Print the information you find. (Write your name on the printout.)
   e. Close the Help window.

4. Use the Layers palette.
   a. Drag the Wine Glasses layer so it is above the Zenith layer.
   b. Use the eye button to hide the Wine Glasses layer.
   c. Make the Wine Glasses layer visible again.
   d. Hide the Zenith layer.
   e. Show the Zenith layer.
   f. Click the Tag Line layer. Notice that the Tag Line layer is now the active layer.
   g. Save your work.

5. View and print an image.
   a. Make sure that all the layers appear in the Layers palette.
   b. Click the Zoom Tool, then make sure the setting is selected to resize the window to fit.
   c. Zoom in on the wine glasses twice.
   d. Zoom out to the original perspective.
   e. Include your name by double-clicking the type layer thumbnail T in the Your Name layer, typing your name, then clicking the Move Tool ⊕.
   f. Print one copy of the document.
   g. Save the document.

6. Close a document and exit Photoshop.
   a. Close the Zenith Design Logo file.
   b. Close the Review file.
   c. Exit (Win) or Quit (Mac) Photoshop.

► Independent Challenges

1. As a new Photoshop user, you are comforted knowing that Photoshop's Help system provides definitions, explanations, procedures, and other helpful information. It also includes examples and demonstrations to show how Photoshop features work. Topics include elements such as the work area and palettes, as well as detailed information about Photoshop commands and options.

a. Open Photoshop and open the Photoshop Help Contents window.
b. Click Producing Consistent Color (Photoshop) in the Contents panel.
c. Click the Why Colors Sometimes Don't Match topic.
d. Once you have read this topic, use the left arrow button to return to the previous screen.
e. Click the About Color Management topic.
f. Print the About Color Management topic, then write your name on the printout.

2. A real estate company just hired you. One of your responsibilities is to determine how Photoshop can be used to increase sales and improve the corporate image. In the real estate business, what types of documents could you create using Photoshop?

a. Think of three uses you might have for Photoshop.
b. Write down three possible uses of Photoshop in the real estate business. (*Hint*: Examples include promotion of properties, announcing new listing agents, or advertising an open house.)
c. In each item listed above, describe the possible print materials you could create. (*Hint*: Examples include a flyer describing a property, a marketing piece that promotes agents, or an advertising slick for a magazine.)
d. Be sure to include your name in your descriptions.

3. You're selected as the Java & Jive Coffeehouse Employee of the Month. Being honored in this way inspires you to send out a thank you message to express your gratitude. To make your card interesting, you scan images that can be used in Photoshop.

a. Obtain at least two images: one from a magazine and one photograph.

b. Once you understand how to operate your scanner, scan each image.

c. Save each image (using the .TIF format) as *Image-1* and *Image-2*, respectively, in the location indicated by your instructor.

d. Start Photoshop, then open each image. If necessary, type your name in the images. (*Hint*: Click the Type Tool T on the toolbox, click an area of the image where you want your name to appear, type your name, then click the Move Tool.

e. Print each image.

4. Now that you are somewhat familiar with Photoshop, you want to see what kind of information is available using the Internet. Adobe Systems Incorporated—the manufacturer of Adobe Photoshop—operates a robust, informative Web site. This Web site has important product information, including user tips and feedback that can make you more skillful at using this program. As a Photoshop user, you should become familiar with this site.

a. Connect to the Internet and go to the Adobe Web site at *http://www.adobe.com*.

b. Once at the Adobe home page, click the link for Products, then click the link for Adobe Photoshop 6.0.

c. Look in Support & Training for Tutorials, then find the page with information on adding color to line art.

d. Print the information. Write your name on the printout.

Photoshop 6.0

► Visual Workshop

Open PS A-3 from the drive and folder where your Project Files are stored and save it as *Kitchen World*. Use the skills you learned in this unit to modify the file so it looks like Figure A-20. Include your name in the lower-left corner of the document by double-clicking **T** in the Name layer and typing your name. Click any other layer in the Layers palette to keep the changes you made to the Name layer. Save your work. Print one copy of the document, then Exit (Win) or Quit (Mac) Photoshop.

FIGURE A-20

Incorporating
Color Techniques

Objectives

- ► **Learn color terminology**
- ► **Choose foreground and background colors**
- ► **Modify colors**
- ► **Add a border to a selection**
- ► **Apply a gradient fill**
- ► **Colorize a grayscale image**
- ► **Adjust image settings**
- ► **Balance colors**

When using a graphics program like Photoshop, it is helpful to have some knowledge of color theory and color terminology. Understanding how Photoshop measures, displays, and prints color can be valuable when creating new images, or modifying existing images. Craig Killdahl is a Zenith Design intern who receives a rush job—design an image for The Chili Shop, an exporter of chili peppers. He needs to learn more about basic color theory so he understands how Photoshop treats color, and then he'll be better able to manipulate images.

Learning Color Terminology

Photoshop displays and prints images using specific color modes. A **mode** is the amount of color data that can be stored in a given file format, based on an established model. A **model** determines how pigments combine to produce resulting colors. The color mode determines the color model used to display and print an image. An image shown on your monitor, such as an icon on your desktop, is a **bitmap**, a geometric arrangement of different color dots on a rectangular grid. Each dot, called a **pixel**, represents a color or shade. Bitmapped images are *resolution-dependent* and can lose detail—often demonstrated by a jagged appearance—when highly magnified. When printed, images with higher resolutions tend to show more detail and subtler color transitions than low-resolution images. To better understand color, Craig decides to learn about Photoshop color modes and models.

QuickTip
Displayed colors can vary from monitor to monitor, even with identical color settings.

Displaying and printing images

In Photoshop, color modes are used to determine how to display and print images. Each mode is based on an established model used in color reproduction. Photoshop provides two specialized color modes: bitmap and grayscale. The **bitmap mode** uses black or white color values to represent image pixels, and is a good choice for images with subtle color gradations, such as photographs or painted images. The **grayscale mode** uses up to 256 shades of gray, assigning a brightness value from 0 (black) to 255 (white) to each pixel.

Color reproduction models

Colors are reproduced in Photoshop using common models, and the range of displayed colors, or **gamut**, is shown in Figure B-1. The L*a*b model, shown in Figure B-2, is based on one luminance component and two chromatic components. This mode is used when working with Photo CD images to allow independent editing of the luminance and color values.

QuickTip
The HSB model is used to define a color in the Color palette or Color Picker dialog box, but there is no HSB mode for creating or editing images.

HSB model

Based on the human perception of color, the HSB model, shown in Figure B-3, has three fundamental characteristics: hue, saturation, and brightness. The color reflected from/transmitted through an object is called **hue**. Expressed as a degree (between 0° and 360°), each hue is identified by a color name (such as red or green). **Saturation** (or *chroma*) is the strength or purity of the color, representing the amount of gray in proportion to hue (measured as a percentage from 0% [gray] to 100% [fully saturated]). **Brightness** is the measurement of relative lightness or darkness of a color (measured as a percentage from 0% [black] to 100% [white]).

QuickTip
Color is created by light passing through red, green, and blue phosphors.

RGB model/mode

Most colors in the visible spectrum can be represented by mixing various proportions and intensities of red, green, and blue colored light. The RGB model is shown in Figure B-4. When red, green, and blue overlap, they create cyan, magenta, and yellow. RGB colors are **additive colors**, creating white when combined. Additive colors are used for lighting, video, and computer monitors. When the values of R, G, and B are zero, the result is black; when the values are all 255, the result is white. In Photoshop, each component of the RGB model is assigned an intensity value.

QuickTip
Subtractive (CMY) and additive (RGB) colors are complementary colors; each pair of one creates one of the other.

CMYK model/mode

The light-absorbing quality of ink printed on paper is the basis of the CMYK model. Unlike the RGB model—in which components are *combined* to create new colors—the CMYK model is based on colors being partially *absorbed* as the ink hits the paper, and then partially *reflected* back to your eyes. When combined, cyan, magenta, and yellow absorb all color and produce black. Because color is absorbed, these are considered **subtractive colors**. The CMYK mode—in which the lightest colors are assigned the highest percentages of ink colors—is used in four-color process printing. Converting an RGB image into a CMYK image produces a **color separation**.

FIGURE B-1: Photoshop gamuts

Color gamuts (Photoshop)

A *gamut* is the range of colors that a color system can display or print. The spectrum of colors seen by the human eye is wider than the gamut available in any color model.

Among the color models used in Photoshop, L*a*b has the largest gamut, encompassing all colors in the RGB and CMYK gamuts. Typically, the RGB gamut contains the subset of these colors that can be viewed on a computer or television monitor (which emits red, green, and blue light). Therefore, some colors, such as pure cyan or pure yellow, can't be displayed accurately on a monitor.

The CMYK gamut is smaller, consisting only of colors that can be printed using process-color inks. When colors that cannot be printed are displayed on-screen, they are referred to as out-of-gamut colors—that is, outside the CMYK gamut. (See Identifying out-of-gamut colors [Photoshop].)

A. Lab color gamut B. RGB color gamut C. CMYK color gamut

FIGURE B-2: L*a*b model

L*a*b model

The L*a*b color model is based on the model proposed by the Commission Internationale d'Eclairage (CIE) in 1931 as an international standard for color measurement. In 1976, this model was refined and named CIE L*a*b.

L*a*b color is designed to be *device independent*, creating consistent color regardless of the device (such as a monitor, printer, computer, or scanner) used to create or output the image.

L*a*b color consists of a *luminance* or lightness component (L) and two chromatic components: the *a* component (from green to red) and the *b* component (from blue to yellow).

A. Luminance=100 (white) B. Green to red component C. Blue to yellow component D. Luminance=0 (black)

FIGURE B-3: HSB model

HSB model

Based on the human perception of color, the HSB model describes three fundamental characteristics of color:

- *Hue* is the color reflected from or transmitted through an object. It is measured as a location on the standard color wheel, expressed as a degree between 0° and 360°. In common use, hue is identified by the name of the color such as red, orange, or green.
- *Saturation*, sometimes called *chroma*, is the strength or purity of the color. Saturation represents the amount of gray in proportion to the hue, measured as a percentage from 0% (gray) to 100% (fully saturated). On the standard color wheel, saturation increases from the center to the edge.
- *Brightness* is the relative lightness or darkness of the color, usually measured as a percentage from 0% (black) to 100% (white).

Although you can use the HSB model in Photoshop to define a color in the Color palette or Color Picker dialog box, there is no HSB mode available for creating and editing images.

A. Saturation B. Hue C. Brightness D. All hues

FIGURE B-4: RGB model

RGB model

A large percentage of the visible spectrum can be represented by mixing red, green, and blue (RGB) colored light in various proportions and intensities. Where the colors overlap, they create cyan, magenta, yellow, and white.

Because the RGB colors combine to create white, they are also called *additive colors*. Adding all colors together creates white—that is, all light is transmitted back to the eye. Additive colors are used for lighting, video, and monitors. Your monitor, for example, creates color by emitting light through red, green, and blue phosphors.

Additive colors (RGB)

Working with Color > About color modes and models (Photoshop) > RGB model

Photoshop 6.0

Choosing Foreground and Background Colors

In Photoshop, the **foreground color** is black, by default, and is used to paint, fill, and apply a border to a selection. The **background color** is white, by default, and is used to make gradient fills and fill in areas of an image that have been erased. You can change the foreground and background colors using the Color palette, the Swatches palette, the Color Picker, or the Eyedropper Tool. ✒ Craig opens an existing document containing guides that were created using the rulers. He wants to experiment with ways of changing the foreground color.

Steps

1. Start Photoshop, **open PS B-1** from the drive and folder where your Project Files are stored, then save the file as **Chili Shop**

2. Click the **Default Foreground and Background Colors button** 🔲 on the toolbox, as shown in Figure B-5, click **View** on the menu bar, then click **Show Rulers**, if necessary
   The foreground and background color settings return to their default settings. The horizontal and vertical rulers appear with the last unit of measure chosen, but can be changed to display other units of measure. Rulers help you to define precise areas within an image.

QuickTip

You can right-click (Win) or [Ctrl] click (Mac) a ruler to display a pop-up menu of units of measure.

3. Click **Edit** on the menu bar, point to **Preferences**, then click **Units & Rulers**
   The Preferences dialog box opens. You can make many changes to the Photoshop program using this series of dialog boxes.

4. Click the **Rulers list arrow** in the Preferences dialog box, click **Pixels**, then click **OK**
   The ruler now uses pixels as its unit of measure, as shown in Figure B-6.

QuickTip

You can also double-click each component's text box in the Color palette and type the color values.

5. Click the **Background layer** in the Layers palette, if necessary, click the **Color tab** in the Color palette, then drag each **color slider** in the Color palette to the right until you reach the values shown in Figure B-7

6. Click the **Gradient Tool** 🔲 on the toolbox, then holding the mouse button until the tools list appears, click the **Paint Bucket Tool** 🔲, then click the **image**
   The image background changes to the foreground color you created in the Color palette.

7. Click **Edit** on the menu bar, then click **Undo Paint Bucket**
   The Background layer returns to its original color. Notice that the Set foreground color button on the toolbox retains the color you previously selected. You can also change the foreground color using the Eyedropper Tool 🖊. You can undo your last task by dragging the action in the History palette to the Delete current state button 🗑.

QuickTip

The first measurement refers to the horizontal ruler (H); the second measurement refers to the vertical ruler (V).

8. Click 🖊 on the toolbox, then using the blue guides to help you, click the **image** at **215 H/60 V**
   When you click a point on the image, the color that you click appears in the Set foreground color button on the toolbox. If you can't see the ruler markings, increase the size of the image. You can use the guides to select the area you want to sample. Missing a ruler measurement even slightly can result in your document looking different from those shown. Even using the exact RGB values, your foreground color may vary from the printed figure, and from monitor to monitor.

9. Click 🔲 on the toolbox, click the **image,** then **save** your work
   Compare your document to Figure B-8.

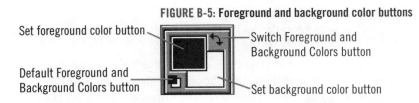

FIGURE B-5: Foreground and background color buttons

Set foreground color button

Switch Foreground and Background Colors button

Default Foreground and Background Colors button

Set background color button

FIGURE B-6: Visible rulers

Your zoom factor may differ

Color tab

Guides

Background layer

Ruler measurement in pixels

FIGURE B-7: New settings in Color palette

Active color selection box

Slider

FIGURE B-8: New foreground color in Background layer

New foreground color

INCORPORATING COLOR TECHNIQUES PHOTOSHOP 29 ◄

Photoshop 6.0

Modifying Colors

In addition to the Color palette and the Eyedropper Tool, you can change colors using the Swatches palette and the Color Picker. The **Swatches palette** contains many colors, and you can also add your own colors to the palette. Depending on the color model you use, you can select colors with the **Color Picker**, a feature that lets you choose a color from a color spectrum, or by numerically defining a custom color. ⬚ Craig likes the current color settings, but wants to explore other methods of changing colors. He starts by examining the Color Picker.

Steps

QuickTip

A circular marker ◯ indicates the active color.

1. Click the **active color selection box** in the Color palette

The Color Picker dialog box opens, as shown in Figure B-9. Make sure that the Hue (H) option button is selected. The color slider displays the range of color levels available for the active color component.

2. Click the **R (Red) option button** in the Color Picker dialog box

The color spectrum changes, displaying the range of color levels available for the red color component. You can change colors in the Color Picker dialog box by dragging the triangles along the vertical color slider, clicking inside the vertical color slider, clicking inside the color field, or entering a value in any text box. The adjustments you make by dragging or clicking on a new color are reflected in the text boxes.

QuickTip

If the out-of-gamut indicator ⚠ appears next to the color, this color exceeds the printable range.

3. Click the **lower-right corner** of the color spectrum (fuchsia)

Notice that the new color appears above the original color, as shown in Figure B-10.

4. Click **Cancel**

The Color Picker dialog box closes, and the foreground color in the Background layer is unchanged.

5. Click the **Swatches palette tab** ⬚ Swatches ⬚

The swatches appear, as shown in Figure B-11. You can use the Swatches palette to choose a color from a visual display. Notice that the pointer changes to ⬚ as it passes over the color swatches.

6. Click the **second swatch from the left in the first row**

The foreground color changes to a lighter, brighter yellow.

7. If necessary, click the **Paint Bucket Tool** ⬚ on the toolbox, then click the **image**

Compare your image to Figure B-12.

QuickTip

To delete a color from the Swatches palette, press [Ctrl] (Win) or [Command] (Mac) while positioning the pointer over a swatch, then click when the pointer turns to ✂.

8. Click the **Eyedropper Tool** ⬚ on the toolbox, click anywhere on the **image background**, click an **empty position** in the last row of the Swatches palette when the pointer turns to ⬚, then click **OK** when the Color Swatch Name dialog box opens

The Background layer color appears in the Swatches palette as a new swatch named Swatch 1. It also appears in the Set foreground color button on the toolbox.

9. Click **File** on the menu bar, then click **Save**

FIGURE B-9: Color Picker dialog box

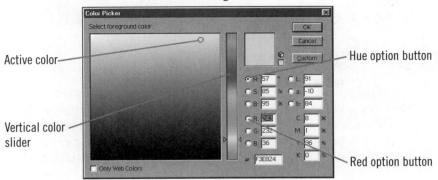

Active color

Vertical color
slider

Hue option button

Red option button

FIGURE B-10: Component changed in Color Picker dialog box

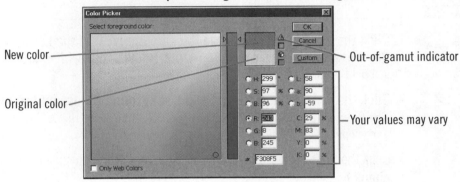

New color

Original color

Out-of-gamut indicator

Your values may vary

FIGURE B-11: Swatches palette

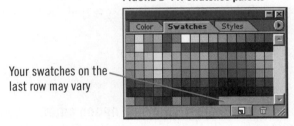

Your swatches on the
last row may vary

FIGURE B-12: Foreground color changed using Swatches palette

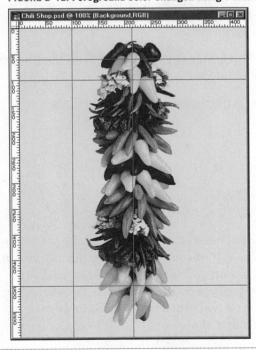

Photoshop 6.0

Adding a Border to a Selection

You can emphasize an image by placing a border along its edges. This process is called **stroking the edges**. Photoshop automatically applies the current foreground color as the border color, unless you select a different color. Craig wants to add a black border around the edges of the chili peppers to make them stand out. Because the peppers are on a separate layer, he begins by hiding the Background layer so it will not be a distraction.

Steps

QuickTip

Use the eye button to hide a distracting layer while working on elements of another layer.

1. Click the **eye button** on the Background layer in the Layers palette
   The Background layer is no longer visible, and the transparent areas of the image appear as a checkerboard.

2. Click the **Default Foreground and Background Colors button** on the toolbox
   The foreground color button on the toolbox changes to black. You want to apply the border to the edges of the chili peppers, not the transparent area.

3. Click the **Chili Peppers layer** in the Layers palette, then click the **Lock transparent pixels check box**
   Compare your screen to Figure B-13. Notice that when you clicked, a lock appeared at the far right on the Chili Peppers layer. This ensures that the transparent areas of the layer remain transparent.

4. Click **Edit** on the menu bar, then click **Stroke**
   The Stroke dialog box appears, as shown in Figure B-14. Your default stroke width value may differ depending on the settings used previously.

QuickTip

Determining the correct border location can be confusing. Try different settings until you get the look you want.

5. Type **3** in the Width text box, click the **Inside option button**, then click **OK**
   A thick black border surrounds the chili peppers. You can also choose a border color using the Color box in the Stroke dialog box. The Location option buttons determine where the border will appear. Clicking the Inside option button caused the border to be placed on the inside edge of the image.

6. Click the **Show/Hide layer button** on the Background layer in the Layers palette
   The Background layer appears, as shown in Figure B-15.

7. Click **File** on the menu bar, then click **Save**

Using guidelines

As you work in Photoshop, you can create an unlimited number of horizontal and vertical guides that help you precisely position elements. If the Snap feature is enabled, you'll feel an object being pulled toward a guide as you drag it on the work area. To turn on the Snap feature, click View on the menu bar, then click Snap. A check mark appears to the left of the command if the feature is enabled. You can create a guide by positioning the mouse pointer on either ruler, then clicking and dragging. As you drag, a guide appears and is positioned on the document when you release the mouse button. You can delete a guide by positioning the pointer over the guide, then clicking and dragging it back to its ruler.

FIGURE B-13: Background layer hidden

Lock transparent
pixels check box

FIGURE B-14: Stroke dialog box

Width

Color

Location options

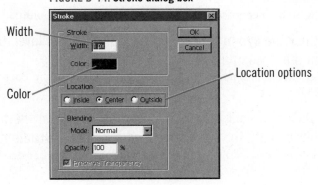

FIGURE B-15: Border added with Background layer shown

Applying a Gradient Fill

You can make colors appear to blend into one another by using a gradient fill. Using one of five gradient tools described in Table B-1, you can create dramatic effects using the gradient fills that come with Photoshop or you can create your own. A gradient's appearance is determined by its beginning and ending points. ✐ Craig wants to change the background color and add a gradient fill effect.

Steps

1. Click the **Eyedropper Tool** 🔧 if necessary, then click ✐ at **245 H/430 V**
   The new foreground color appears on the toolbox.

2. Click the **Switch Foreground and Background Colors button** ⤢ on the toolbox
   The foreground color becomes the background color.

3. Click **Swatch 1** on the Swatches palette *(this is the swatch you added to the Swatches palette in the Modifying Colors lesson)*
   Swatch 1 becomes the foreground color on the toolbox.

4. Click the **eye button** 👁 on the Chili Peppers layer, then click the **Background layer** in the Layers palette
   The Chili Peppers layer no longer appears, and the Background layer is active, as shown in Figure B-16.

5. Click and hold the **Paint Bucket Tool** 🪣 on the toolbox, then holding the mouse button until the tools list appears, click the **Gradient Tool** ▨
   The pointer changes to -┼-, and the tool options bar displays the five gradient tools listed in Table B-1.

6. Click the **Click to open Gradient picker list arrow** to open the Gradient pop-up palette, as shown in figure B-17, then click **Foreground to Background** *(the first gradient fill in the first row)*

7. Click the **Click to open Gradient picker list arrow** again to close the pop-up palette, then drag -┼- from **100 H/60 V** to **215 H/500 V** in the document window
   The gradient fill appears in the document window. The length, direction, and angle of a gradient fill are determined by the length, direction, and angle of the temporary line that appears as you drag -┼- across the image.

8. Click the **Show/Hide layer button** ▢ on the **Chili Peppers layer** in the Layers palette
   The Chili Peppers layer appears, as shown in Figure B-18, with the gradient fill in the background.

9. Click **File** on the menu bar, then click **Save**
   It is a good idea to save your work early and often in the creation process, especially before making significant changes or printing.

FIGURE B-16: **Chili Peppers layer hidden**

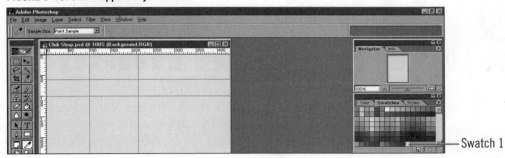

Swatch 1

FIGURE B-17: **Gradient pop-up palette**

Tool options bar displaying gradient tools

Gradient options

Gradient pop-up palette

FIGURE B-18: **Gradient fill in Background layer**

TABLE B-1: **Gradient tools and descriptions**

tool	tool name	description
	Linear gradient	Creates a straight-line pattern from starting to ending point
	Radial gradient	Creates a circular pattern from starting to ending point
	Angle gradient	Creates a counterclockwise pattern around the starting point
	Reflected gradient	Creates symmetrical patterns on either side of the starting point
	Diamond gradient	Creates a pattern from the starting point outward

Colorizing a Grayscale Image

A grayscale image can contain as many as 256 shades of gray. Within an image, pixels have a brightness value from 0 (black) to white (255). When a color image is converted to grayscale, the light and dark values—called the **luminosity**—remain, while the color information is deleted. Once converted to grayscale, an image can be colorized by adjusting its hue, saturation, and lightness (brightness). ⬤▬ Craig already created a grayscale image for the Chili Shop design. Now he wants to colorize the image and experiment with a variety of effects.

Steps

QuickTip

Any bitmap-mode or color image can be converted to a grayscale image by clicking Image on the menu bar, pointing to Mode, then clicking to Grayscale.

1. **Open PS B-2** from the drive and folder where your Project Files are stored, then save the file as **Chili Shop Colorized**
   The new document appears over the Chili Shop document. Compare your screen to Figure B-19.

2. Click **Image** on the menu bar, point to **Mode**, then click **RGB Color**
   Notice that (RGB) appears on the document title bar, and the Swatches palette and toolbox foreground and background buttons are in color.

3. Click **Image** on the menu bar, point to **Adjust**, then click **Hue/Saturation**
   The Hue/Saturation dialog box opens, as shown in Figure B-20.

Trouble?

If you drag the slider and the color does not change, make sure the Preview check box is checked, then wait a few seconds for the new color to appear.

4. Click the **Colorize check box** in the Hue/Saturation dialog box
   Notice that the image now has a brownish tint, which can be changed to another color by dragging the Hue slider in the Hue/Saturation dialog box. You can also type a value in the Hue text box.

5. Drag the **Hue slider** until the text box displays **+ 240**
   The image is now light purple.

6. Drag the **Saturation slider** until the text box displays **+ 45**
   The light purple color intensifies.

7. Drag the **Lightness slider** until the text box displays **+10**, then click **OK**
   The purple color deepens as the image gets darker. Compare your image to Figure B-21.

8. Click **File** on the menu bar, then click **Save**

FIGURE B-19: Grayscale image

New foreground
and background
colors

FIGURE B-20: Hue/Saturation dialog box

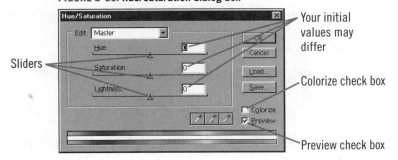

Sliders

Your initial
values may
differ

Colorize check box

Preview check box

FIGURE B-21: Colorized image

Photoshop 6.0

Adjusting Image Settings

It is often difficult to know when a document is finished. As with any project, you can always make tweaks here and there. You may want to adjust an image's contrast and sharpness. Photoshop has special features called filters, such as the **Sharpen More filter**, which increases the contrast of adjacent pixels, and can focus blurry images. A **blending mode** can darken or lighten colors, depending on which ones are in use, by controlling the effect of a painting or editing tool on pixels. **Opacity** affects an image's transparency. Craig wants to put some final touches on the image. He begins by adjusting the contrast.

Trouble?

Make sure the Preview check box is selected. If it is deselected, you will not see the changes you made to the image until you click OK.

1. Click **Image** on the menu bar, point to **Adjust**, then click **Brightness/Contrast**

   The Brightness/Contrast dialog box opens, as shown in Figure B-22. You can change either or both settings.

2. Drag the **Brightness slider** until **+15** appears in the Brightness text box, drag the **Contrast slider** until **+25** appears in the Contrast text box, then click **OK**

   The brightness and contrast between light and dark objects are increased. You can use the Sharpen More filter to add contrast.

3. Click **Filter** on the menu bar, point to **Sharpen**, then click **Sharpen More**

   The image border and features become more pronounced. You can adjust the sharpness using the Fade Sharpen More command.

4. Click **Edit** on the menu bar, then click **Fade Sharpen More**

   The Fade dialog box opens, as shown in Figure B-23.

5. Drag the **Opacity slider** until **55** appears in the Opacity text box

6. Click the **Mode list arrow**, click **Dissolve**, then click **OK**

   The Dissolve mode makes colors look more like their surrounding pixels. Compare your image to Figure B-24.

7. Click **File** on the menu bar, then click **Save**

Understanding color channels

A **color channel** is an area where color information is stored. A Photoshop image has at least one color channel in the Channels palette. Each channel stores the color information for that image. The default number of channels is determined by an image's color mode. A grayscale image contains a single channel, while RGB and L*a*b images each have three channels, in addition to a composite channel. The maximum number of channels is 24. You can add channels to all color modes, except the bitmap mode.

FIGURE B-22: Brightness/Contrast dialog box

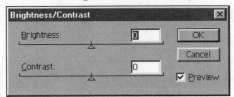

FIGURE B-23: Fade dialog box

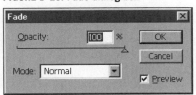

FIGURE B-24: Image settings adjusted

Balancing Colors

As you adjust settings, such as hue and saturation, you may create imbalances in your document that affect overall appearance. You can adjust colors to correct or improve a document's appearance. A color can be decreased by increasing the amount of its opposite color. Using the color wheel in Figure B-25 as a guide, you can increase or decrease a color by adjusting two adjacent colors on the wheel, or you can adjust two adjacent colors of that color's opposite. Craig wants to balance the colors in the Chili Shop image.

Steps

QuickTip

In addition to the filename, all of the image information contained on the document title bar appears on the Window menu.

1. Click **Window** on the menu bar, then click **Chili Shop.psd (Win)** or **Chili Shop (Mac)**
   The original image appears in front of the colorized image.

2. Click **Image** on the menu bar, point to **Adjust**, then click **Color Balance**
   The Color Balance dialog box opens. You can drag each slider to adjust the color components.

3. Drag the **Cyan-Red slider** until **+20** appears in the first text box
   Moving the slider away from cyan creates a more red appearance.

4. Drag the **Magenta-Green slider** until **-30** appears in the middle text box
   More magenta is added to the image.

5. Drag the **Yellow-Blue slider** until **+20** appears in the last text box, as shown in Figure B-26, then click **OK**

6. Type your name in the lower-left corner of the document (*Hint*: Click the **Type Tool** T on the toolbox, click the lower-left corner of the document, then type your name)
   Your name will appear on a new layer in the Layers palette. Click any other layer in the Layers palette to keep the changes you just made to the new layer.

7. Click **File** on the menu bar, then click **Save**
   Compare your finished project with Figure B-27.

8. Click **File** on the menu bar, click **Print**, then click **OK**

9. Click the **Swatches list arrow** ⊙ in the Swatches palette, click **Reset Swatches**, click **OK**, then **Exit (Win)** or **Quit (Mac)** Photoshop

FIGURE B-25: Color wheel

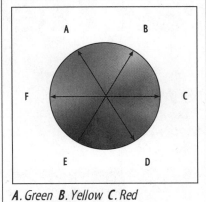

A. Green B. Yellow C. Red
D. Magenta E. Blue F. Cyan

FIGURE B-26: Color Balance dialog box settings

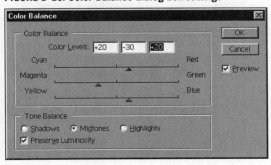

FIGURE B-27: Completed image

Swatches list arrow

Photoshop 6.0

Practice

► Concepts Review

Label each element in the Photoshop window shown in Figure B-28.

FIGURE B-28

Match each button, tool, or pointer with the statement that describes its function.

7. Samples colors
8. Fills an area with color
9. Creates a linear gradient
10. Creates a diamond gradient
11. Creates an angle gradient
12. Displays available colors

a. [icon]
b. [icon]
c. [icon]
d. Swatches
e. [icon]
f. [icon]

Select the best answer from the list of choices.

13. Which tool is used to make colors appear to blend?
    a.
    b.
    c.
    d.

14. What color is used to paint, fill, and stroke a selection?
    a. Normal
    b. Foreground
    c. Moderate
    d. Background

15. Which symbol appears when a color exceeds the printable range?
    a.
    b.
    c.
    d.

16. Which pointer appears when you add a color to the Swatches palette?
    a.
    b.
    c.
    d.

17. Rulers can be turned on using which menu?
    a. Edit
    b. Image
    c. View
    d. Window

18. Which mode uses black or white color values to represent image pixels?
    a. RGB
    b. Lab
    c. Grayscale
    d. Bitmap

19. RGB colors create white when combined, and are
    a. Subtractive.
    b. Cautionary.
    c. Separate.
    d. Additive.

20. Converting an RGB image into a CMYK image produces a

    a. Color spectrum.

    b. Color field.

    c. Color switch.

    d. Color separation.

21. Which color model is based on partial absorption of the spectrum?

    a. Bitmap

    b. RGB

    c. CMYK

    d. Grayscale

Skills Review

1. Choose foreground and background colors.

    a. Start Photoshop.

    b. Open PS B-3 from the drive and folder where your Project Files are stored, then save it as *Firetruck*.

    c. Make sure the rulers appear (using pixels), and the foreground and background colors are set to default.

    d. Use the Eyedropper Tool to sample the color at 90 H/165 V.

    e. Use the Paint Bucket Tool to apply the new foreground color to the Background layer.

    f. Undo the paint bucket effect.

    g. Switch the foreground and background colors.

2. Modify colors.

    a. Open the Color Picker dialog box.

    b. One at a time, click the R, G, and B option buttons. Note how the Color palette changes.

    c. With the B option button selected, click the palette in the upper-left corner (aqua).

    d. Click OK.

    e. Switch the foreground and background colors.

    f. Add the foreground color (red) to the Swatches palette.

3. Add a border to a selection.

    a. Activate Layer 1.

    b. Revert to the default foreground and background colors.

    c. Apply a 2-pixel outside stroke to the fire truck.

    d. Save your work.

4. Apply a gradient fill.

    a. Make the foreground color the eighth swatch from the left in the top row.

    b. Switch foreground and background colors.

    c. Make the foreground color the red color box on the Swatches palette (added in step 2F).

    d. Activate the Background layer.

    e. Click the Angle Gradient Tool, then drag the pointer from 35 H/70 V to 145 H/325 V.

    f. Save your work.

5. Colorize a grayscale image.

   a. Open PS B-4, then save it as *Firetruck Colorized*.

   b. Modify the mode to RGB Color.

   c. Open the Hue/Saturation dialog box, then click Colorize.

   d. Drag the sliders so the text boxes show the following values: +25, +75, and +15.

   e. Save your work.

6. Adjust image settings.

   a. Use the Filter menu to sharpen the image. (Use the Sharpen command.)

   b. Open the Fade dialog box (Edit Menu), change the opacity to 40%, then change the mode to Hard Light.

   c. Save your work.

7. Balance colors.

   a. Use the Window menu to activate the Firetruck.psd image.

   b. Open the Color Balance dialog box.

   c. Change the color level settings so the text boxes show the following values: +61, -15, and +40.

   d. Type your name in the lower-left corner of the document. (*Hint*: Click the Type Tool ⊤ on the toolbox, click an area of the image where you want your name to appear, type your name, then click another layer in the Layers palette to keep the changes you made to the new layer.)

   e. Save your work.

   f. Exit (Win) or Quit (Mac) Photoshop.

► Independent Challenges

1. You are finally able to leave your current job, and pursue your lifelong dream of opening a furniture restoration business. While you're waiting for the laser stripper and refinisher to arrive, you can start work on a sign design.

   a. Open PS B-5, then save it as *Furniture*.

   b. Use your knowledge of foreground and background colors to create a background that conveys the right feel for upscale antique furniture.

   c. Change the foreground and background colors as necessary.

   d. Use a gradient tool to create an interesting effect on the Background layer.

   e. Type your name in the lower-left corner of the document. (*Hint*: Click the Type Tool ⊤ on the toolbox, click on the image where you want your name to appear, type your name, then click another layer in the Layers palette to keep the changes you made to the new layer.)

   f. Save and print the image.

2. You're repairing some classic Art Deco cabinets at a private preschool. You notice that a staff member is struggling to create a newspaper ad for the school, so you offer to help.

a. Open PS B-6, then save it as *Preschool*.
b. Make the Background layer active, then experiment with effects that suggest a fun but nurturing atmosphere that you think would attract clients.
c. Change the foreground and background colors as necessary.
d. Use a gradient tool to create an interesting effect on the Background layer.
e. Type your name in the lower-left corner of the document. (*Hint*: Click the Type Tool [T] on the toolbox, type your name, then click another layer in the Layers palette.)
f. Save and print the image.

3. You can find unique colors in print ads. Find at least two color print ads or images that use interesting colors.

a. Obtain at least two color print ads or images.
b. Scan each image.
c. Save the images as *Ad-1* and *Ad-2* (using the .TIF format) in the drive and folder where your Project Files are stored.
d. Start Photoshop, then open each image.
e. Use the Eyedropper Tool to sample at least one interesting color from each image, and add them to the Swatches palette.
f. Create a Photoshop document using the size 325 pixels × 325 pixels, then save the file as *New Colors* in the drive and folder where your Project Files are stored.
g. Use the new colors (with a gradient tool) on the Background layer to create an interesting effect.
h. Type your name in the lower-left corner of the document. (*Hint*: Click the Type Tool [T] on the toolbox, type your name, then click another layer in the Layers palette.)
i. Print, then save and close the image.

4. A gradient fill effect adds a professional quality to any design. Why is this effect so dramatic? Can any colors be used in a gradient fill? How should you choose these colors? When can this effect become counterproductive? You can find answers to these questions by looking at print ads and images, examining backgrounds used on the web, or searching the web for more information. To complete this independent challenge:

a. Go to the Google search engine at *http://www.google.com* and enter: "Photoshop color modes." You can also use Yahoo!, Excite, Infoseek, or another search engine of your choice.

b. Use any of the links to find information about color. (*Hint:* You may have to visit more than one site to get all the information you need.)

c. Print out pages containing any relevant information you find on this topic.

d. Open a new document in your favorite word processor, then save it as *Color Modes* in the location where your Project Files are stored.

e. Write a maximum of one-page that discusses Photoshop's color modes and the best application for each.

f. Include your name within the document, then save and print this file.

g. Exit the word processor.

▶ Visual Workshop

Open PS B-7 from the drive and folder where your Project Files are stored, and save it as *Cornucopia*. Use the skills you learned in this unit to modify the document so it looks like Figure B-29. Use the Eyedropper Tool to obtain colors for the foreground and background. Take a sample at 420 H/360 V and at 200 H/330 V. Use the Linear Gradient Tool and draw a line from 100 H/100 V to 500 H/500 V. Type your name in the lower-left corner of the document. (*Hint*: Click the Type Tool **T** on the toolbox, type your name, then click another layer in the Layers palette.) Save and print the image.

FIGURE B-29

Photoshop 6.0

Placing
Type in an Image

Objectives

► **Understand type fundamentals**
► **Create type**
► **Modify type**
► **Create a drop shadow**
► **Change a font and apply anti-aliasing**
► **Apply the Bevel and Emboss style to type**
► **Use filters with type**
► **Apply a filter to type**

Text can play an important role when used along with images, such as in magazine and newspaper advertisements. In Photoshop, text is referred to as **type**. There are many ways to manipulate type in Photoshop in order to convey or reinforce the meaning behind an image. As with other programs, type has its own unique characteristics in Photoshop. Erin Murphy is an account executive at Zenith Design. She will be conducting a seminar on using type in Photoshop for the company's interns.

Understanding Type Fundamentals

Outline type is mathematically defined and can be scaled to any size without its edges losing their smooth appearance. Some programs, such as Adobe Illustrator, create outline type. **Bitmap type** is composed of pixels, and, like images, may develop jagged edges when enlarged. The type you create in Photoshop is initially outline type, but it is converted into bitmap type when special filters are applied. Using the tool options bar, you can create horizontal or vertical type, and modify font size, alignment, and color. When you create type in Photoshop, it is automatically placed on a new type layer in the Layers palette. Keeping type on separate type layers makes it much easier to manipulate it. Before showing the interns how to create type in Photoshop, Erin reviews some type fundamentals.

QuickTip

The fonts available on each computer may vary.

Font families

Each **font family** represents a complete set of characters, letters, and symbols for a particular typeface. Font families are generally divided into three categories: serif, sans serif, and symbol. Some characters in **serif fonts** have a tail, or stroke, at the end. These tails make it easier for the eye to recognize words. For this reason, serif fonts are generally used in text passages. **Sans serif fonts** do not have tails and are commonly used in headlines. **Symbol fonts** are used to display unique characters (such as $, ÷, or ™). Table C-1 lists commonly used serif and sans serif fonts.

Type size and measurement units

The size of each character within a font is measured in **points**. **PostScript**, a programming language that optimizes printed text and graphics, was introduced by Adobe in 1985. In PostScript measurement, 1 inch is equivalent to 72 points or 6 picas. Therefore, 1 pica is equivalent to 12 points. In traditional measurement, 1 inch is equivalent to 72.27 points. The default Photoshop type size is 12 points. In Photoshop, you have the option of using PostScript or traditional character measurement. To prevent the jagged edges that often characterize bitmap type, Photoshop offers an anti-aliasing feature. **Anti-aliasing** partially fills in pixel edges, resulting in smooth-edge type. Anti-aliasing improves the display of large type in print media.

Line and character spacing

Between characters and lines type spacing can be controlled. Fonts in desktop publishing and word processing programs use proportional spacing, whereas typewriters use monotype spacing. In **monotype spacing**, each character occupies the same amount of space. This means that characters such as "o" and "w" take up the same area as "i" and "l." In **proportional spacing**, each character may take up a different amount of space, depending on its width. **Kerning** is the ability to control the amount of space between two characters. **Tracking** inserts a *uniform* amount of space between characters. Tracking and kerning can be performed manually or automatically in Photoshop by using the Character palette. The amount of space between lines of type, or **leading**, lets you add or decrease the distance between lines.

Type styles

Type styles, including drop shadows, glows, beveling, and embossing, can greatly enhance the appearance of type. Figure C-1 shows a document with several type layers and styles. A type layer is indicated by the appearance of the T icon T in the layer's thumbnail. When one or more styles are applied to type, an "f" icon, called the Layer style button appears on that layer when it is active. The Layer style button appears as ▶ ● when the layer is inactive. Type layer buttons used in the Macintosh version of Photoshop are similar to those found in the Windows version. Layer styles are linked to the contents of a layer, which means that if a type layer is moved or modified, the layer's style will still be applied to the type.

FIGURE C-1: Document with multiple type layers

Thumbnail box

Type layer

TABLE C-1: Commonly used serif and sans serif fonts

serif fonts	sample	sans serif fonts	sample
Lucida Handwriting	*Adobe Photoshop*	Arial	Adobe Photoshop
Rockwell	**Adobe Photoshop**	Bauhaus	**Adobe Photoshop**
Times New Roman	Adobe Photoshop	Century Gothic	Adobe Photoshop

CLUES TO USE

Using the active layer palette background (Macintosh)

Icons used in Macintosh to identify type layers are similar to those found in Windows. The active layer, shown in Figure C-2, has the same Type T and Layer style buttons ▷ ⬤. In Macintosh, the active layer's background color is the same color as the Highlight Color chosen in the Appearance control panel menu item. (In Windows, the active layer's background color is navy blue.)

FIGURE C-2: Layers palette (Mac)

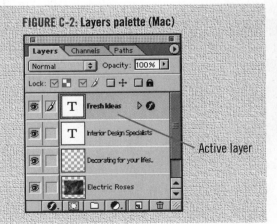

Active layer

Photoshop 6.0

Photoshop 6.0

Steps

Creating Type

The type that you create in Photoshop is typically used with imagery to quickly deliver a message with flair. Because type is used sparingly, its appearance is important. Color and imagery are often used to complement or reinforce a message within the text. Type should be short in length, but direct and to the point. It should be large enough for easy reading, but should not overwhelm or distract from the central image. ✎ Erin prepared an image for a print ad for Fresh Ideas, an interior design firm. She will add a type layer to the image to convey a positive message about the company.

1. Start Photoshop, open **PS C-1** from the drive and folder where your Project Files are stored, then save the file as **Fresh Ideas**

2. Click the **Default Foreground and Background Colors button** ▣ on the toolbox
   The foreground and background colors now display the default settings.

Trouble?

If rulers do not appear, click View on the menu bar, then click Show Rulers.

3. Click the **Type Tool** T on the toolbox, the pointer changes to ⌶, click the **Set the font size list arrow** `60 pt ▾` on the tool options bar, click **60**, then click the **Left align text button** ≣ on the tool options bar
   When you click T, new buttons appear on the tool options bar, as shown in Figure C-3. The initial values on your tool options bar may differ. The tool options bar makes it easy to adjust type settings. You can also double-click a type layer's thumbnail to show the Type Tool options on the tool options bar.

4. Click the **Set the text color button** ▣ on the tool options bar
   The Color Picker dialog box opens.

Trouble?

Drag the Color Picker dialog box out of the way if it blocks your view of the image.

5. Click 🖋 at **60 H/370 V**, then click **OK** in the Color Picker dialog box
   When you want to use a color that exists in the image, you can click that particular point on the image. The sampled color appears on the tool options bar, and becomes the new type color.

Trouble?

If you click on the wrong spot, move on to the next step. You will be able to move your text after you create it.

6. Click the **Set the font family list arrow** on the tool options bar, click **Times New Roman**, if necessary, then click at **240 H/ 90 V**
   Refer to Figure C-3.

7. Type **Fresh Ideas**, then click the **Move Tool** ⊹ on the toolbox
   The new layer appears on the Layers palette as Fresh Ideas. See Figure C-4. When you finish typing, the text cursor continues flashing in the work area, preventing you from performing any other Photoshop tasks. To save or exit the program, click either another tool on the toolbox, or another layer in the Layers palette. It makes sense to click the Move Tool so that you can move the type, if desired.

Trouble?

If you cannot move a layer, make sure it is active.

8. Drag **Fresh Ideas** with ⊹, if necessary, so that it is in approximately the same location shown in Figure C-4, then **save** your work

9. Click **File** on the menu bar, then click **Save**

FIGURE C-3: Tool options bar with Type Tool settings

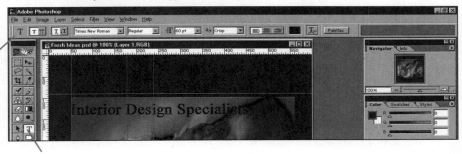

Tool options bar
with Type Tool
buttons

Type Tool

FIGURE C-4: New type layer in image

New type in image

Layer thumbnail

New type layer

 Using the Navigator palette

You can change the magnification factor of an image using the Navigator palette or the Zoom Tool on the toolbox. By double-clicking the Zoom box 200% in the Navigator palette, you can enter a new magnification factor, then press [Enter] (Win) or [Return] (Mac). Figure C-5 shows the Navigator palette with a zoom factor of 225%. The red border in the palette, called the Proxy Preview Area, defines the area of the magnified image. You can drag the Proxy Preview Area inside the Navigator palette to view other areas of the image at the current magnification factor.

FIGURE C-5: Enlarged area in Navigator palette

Magnification factor

Enlarged area of the document

Photoshop 6.0

Modifying Type

You already know that you can change type color by taking a sample from the current image using the Eyedropper Tool. You can also use the Color Picker dialog box to select a type color. By default, type color initially appears in the current foreground color on the toolbox. The **Character palette**, which is accessed through the tool options bar, helps you control type properties, such as kerning, tracking, and leading. Type rests on an invisible line called a **baseline**. Using the Character palette, you can adjust the **baseline shift**, the vertical distance that type moves from its baseline. ━━ Erin wants to modify the existing type layers. She uses the Character palette to adjust various characteristics of the type.

Steps

1. Double-click the **Type layer button 'T'** on the **Interior Design Specialists layer** on the Layers palette, then click the **Show the Character & Paragraph palettes button** `Palettes` on the tool options bar
   The Character palette opens, as shown in Figure C-6. You can add some space between the letters "r" and "i" in "Interior" by kerning these letters. Positive kerning values add space between characters, while negative values decrease space between characters.

2. Click ↧ **between "r" and "i"** in the word "Interior" so that you see a flashing cursor, click the **Set the kerning between two characters list arrow** in the Character palette, then click **25**
   Additional space appears between the letters "r" and "i."

3. Press **[Ctrl][A] (Win)** or **[Command][A] (Mac)** to select all the text on the Interior Design Specialists layer
   Now you can change the type color using the Color Picker dialog box.

QuickTip

Clicking the Set the text color button opens the Color Picker dialog box.

4. Click the **Set the text color button** ▦ on the tool options bar
   The Color Picker dialog box opens. You can change colors by clicking the color slider, then clicking a color in the color spectrum.

QuickTip

You may notice that when you click yellow in the color spectrum, the active layer type changes color, although your colors may vary.

5. If necessary, click the **H (Hue) option button** in the Color Picker dialog box, click yellow in the color slider, click ○ in the upper-right corner of the color spectrum, as shown in Figure C-7, then click **OK**
   The type color changes; however, you won't see the new color while the text is selected. The foreground color on the Character palette and on the tool options bar changes to yellow.

6. Select the **capital "I" in "Interior"** using ↧, double-click **35** in the **Set the font size text box** in the Character palette, type **40**, double-click **0** in the **Set the baseline shift text box** in the Character palette, then type **-5**
   Notice that the "I" is larger and drops slightly below the remaining type.

7. Select **"D" in "Design"** using ↧, double-click the **Set the font size text box**, type **40**, double-click the **Set the baseline text box**, type **-5**, select **"S" in "Specialists"** using ↧, double-click the **Set the font size text box**, type **40**, double-click the **Set the baseline shift text box**, type **-5**, click the **Commit any current edits button** ☑ on the tool options bar, then close the Character palette
   The first letter of the words on the active type layer is larger and lower.

Trouble?

If you do not see the 550 vertical mark on the ruler, resize your document window.

8. Click the **Move Tool** ▶⊕ on the toolbox, if necessary, position the ▶⊕ over the "I" in "Interior," then drag the text to **50 H/550 V**, as shown in Figure C-8

9. Click **File** on the menu bar, then click **Save**

FIGURE C-6: Character palette

Character palette

Selected type

FIGURE C-7: Color Picker dialog box

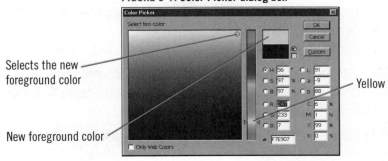

Selects the new foreground color

New foreground color

Yellow

FIGURE C-8: Modified type layer

Character with baseline shift adjustment

CLUES TO USE

Using the Eyedropper Tool to change type color

Using the Color Picker is only one method of changing type color. You can also select colors from the Swatches palette, or use the Eyedropper Tool to sample colors from an image. When the Eyedropper Tool is active, the pointer changes to 🔍 when it's positioned over the image or the Swatches palette. If you click a swatch in the Swatches palette, or click the image, the new color you clicked will appear in the Set foreground color button on the toolbox and be applied to type currently selected.

Creating a Drop Shadow

One method of emphasizing type is to add a drop shadow to it. A **drop shadow** creates an illusion that another colored layer of identical text is behind the selected type. The drop shadow default color is black, but can be changed to another color using the Color Picker dialog box, or any of the other methods for changing color. You can control many aspects of a drop shadow's appearance, including its angle, distance behind the type, and amount of blur it contains. ⬥ Erin wants to add a drop shadow to a type layer. First, she changes the type color to make it more visible.

1. Double-click the **Type layer button** T on the **Decorating for your lifestyle layer** in the Layers palette

   The tool options bar displays Type Tool settings, and all the text on the layer is selected.

2. Click the **Set the text color button** on the tool options bar, click 🖉 in the **Set foreground color button** on the toolbox ▣, click **OK**, then click the **Move Tool** ➤₊

   The type on the active layer appears in yellow.

QuickTip

You can also open the Layer Style dialog box by double-clicking a layer in the Layers palette.

3. Click **Layer** on the menu bar, point to **Layer Style**, then click **Drop Shadow**

   The Layer Style dialog box opens.

4. Double-click the **Angle text box**, type **150**, double-click the **Distance text box**, then type **10**

   Compare your settings to those shown in Figure C-9. You can also set the angle by dragging the dial slider in the Layer Style dialog box. The Drop Shadow settings are shown in the Layer Style dialog box's preview window.

5. Click **OK**

   Notice that a shadow appears behind the text and the Layer style button ▣🗇 appears on the Decorating for your lifestyle layer. You can view the list of styles applied to a type layer in more detail using the Layers palette. See Figure C-10.

6. Click the **Show/Hide layer style button** ▶ on the **Decorating for your lifestyle layer**

   Compare your Layers palette to Figure C-10. The Drop Shadow is listed under the Effects bar.

7. Click the **Show/Hide layer style button** ▼ again on the **Decorating for your lifestyle layer** to close the list and show more of the Layers palette

   Compare your document to Figure C-11.

8. Click **File** on the menu bar, then click **Save**

Filling type with imagery

You can use the imagery from a layer in one file as the fill pattern for another image's type layer. To create this effect, open a multi-layer file that contains the imagery you want to use (the source), then open the file that contains the type you want to fill (the target). In the source file, activate the layer containing the imagery you want to use, use the Select menu to select all, then use the Edit menu to copy the selection. In the target file, press [Ctrl] while clicking the type layer to which the imagery will be applied, then click Paste Into on the Edit menu. The imagery will appear within the type.

FIGURE C-9: Layer Style dialog box

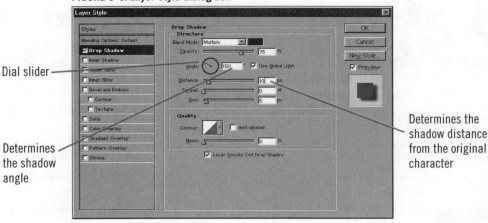

Dial slider

Determines the shadow angle

Determines the shadow distance from the original character

FIGURE C-10: Effects detail in Layers palette

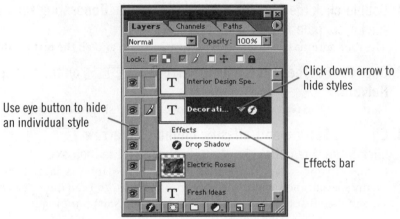

Use eye button to hide an individual style

Click down arrow to hide styles

Effects bar

FIGURE C-11: Drop Shadow added to type layer

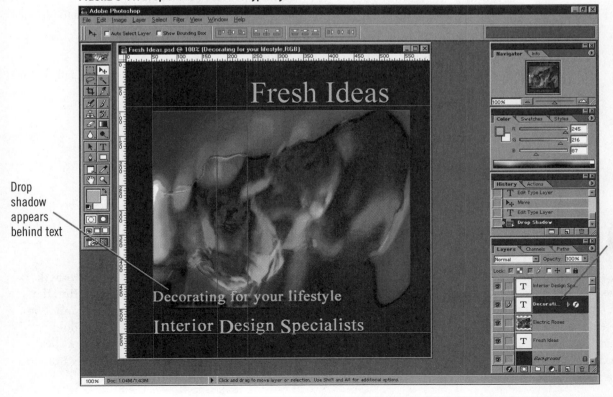

Drop shadow appears behind text

Layer effects icon

Photoshop 6.0

Photoshop 6.0

Changing a Font and Applying Anti-aliasing

As stated earlier, **anti-aliasing** is a Photoshop feature that partially fills in pixel edges, resulting in smooth-edge type. Anti-aliasing improves the display of type against the background. There are four anti-aliasing methods: None, Sharp, Strong, and Crisp. The **Crisp** setting gives type more definition and makes it appear sharper. You can experiment with type by changing the font, adding type styles, and applying anti-aliasing methods. You'll find that the appearance of type style can help convey a message. Generally, the type used in your image should be the messenger, not the message. As you work with type, keep in mind that using more than two fonts in one document may make the overall appearance look unprofessional or distracting. ✎ Erin wants to experiment with changing the type font and anti-aliasing method.

Steps 1 2 3 4

1. Double-click the **Type layer button** T on the **Decorating for your lifestyle layer** in the Layers palette
   The tool options bar displays Type Tool settings, and all the text on the layer is selected.

Trouble?

If you do not see Helvetica in your list of fonts, choose a similar font, such as Arial.

2. Click the **Set the font family list arrow** `Times New Roman ▾` on the tool options bar, then click **Helvetica**
   Notice that the type changes in the document, as shown in Figure C-12.

3. Click the **Set the anti-aliasing method list arrow** `Crisp ▾` on the tool options bar, click **None**, then click the **Move Tool** ▶₊ on the toolbox
   Compare your screen to Figure C-13. The type appears jagged, the characters are more evenly spaced, and the text looks less professional. You can undo the changes by dragging the state in the History palette to the Delete current state button 🗑.

4. Click the **Edit Type Layer** state in the History palette, then drag it to the 🗑
   As you drag the History state to 🗑, the pointer becomes ⟨⟩, and the state turns yellow, as shown in Figure C-14. Once the state is deleted, the type returns to its original appearance.

5. Click **File** on the menu bar, then click **Save**
   It is a good idea to save your work early and often in the creation process, especially before making significant changes or printing.

Warping type

You can add dimension and style to your type by using the Warp Text feature. Once you have selected the type layer you want to warp, click T on the toolbox. Click the Create warped text button ⊤₌ on the tool options bar and the Warp Text dialog box opens. You can click the Style list arrow to select from 15 available styles. Once you select a style, you can modify its appearance by dragging the Bend, Horizontal Distortion, and Vertical Distortion sliders. (Hint: If a warning box opens telling you your request cannot be completed because the type layer uses a faux bold style, click `Palettes` on the tool options bar, click the Character palette list arrow ▸, click Faux Bold to deselect it, then click ⊤₌ again.)

FIGURE C-12: Font changed

Font family list arrow   Anti-aliasing method list arrow

FIGURE C-13: Effect of anti-alias feature

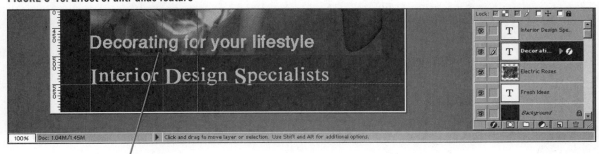

Type may appear jagged if you choose
None as the anti-aliasing method

FIGURE C-14: Deleting a state from the History palette

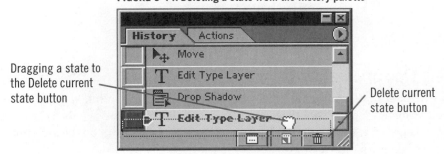

Dragging a state to
the Delete current
state button

Delete current
state button

Applying the Bevel and Emboss Style to Type

The Bevel and Emboss style is used to add combinations of shadows and highlights to a layer, and can give type a more professional appearance. Like all type styles, the Bevel and Emboss style is linked to the type layer to which it is applied. When type is moved or edited, the style is also modified. Like the Drop Shadow style, you can control the angle, depth, and blur of the Bevel and Emboss style, allowing you to create a truly unique appearance. Erin wants to add the Bevel style to some type to add dimension to a type layer.

Steps

1. Click the Fresh Ideas layer in the Layers palette
You can apply more than one style to an active layer.

Trouble?

If you do not see the Style list arrow in the Layer Style dialog box, click the Bevel and Emboss check box in the Styles pane of the Layer Style dialog box.

2. Click Layer on the menu bar, point to Layer Style, then click Bevel and Emboss
The Layer Style dialog box opens, as shown in Figure C-15. Once the dialog box opens, the type changes to reflect the current settings in the dialog box. You can choose a bevel *or* emboss style from the Style list arrow in the Layer Style dialog box.

3. If necessary, move the Layer Style dialog box so you can see the Fresh Ideas type

4. Double-click the Angle text box, then type 135
The Angle setting determines the direction of the bevel. The text takes on a more angular appearance, and light appears to be coming from the left.

5. Double-click the Altitude text box, then type 40
Now the text appears to have more depth. Altitude values can range from 0 to 90. An altitude of 0 looks flat, while a setting of 90 has a more three-dimensional appearance. Compare your settings to Figure C-16.

6. Click OK
Compare your screen to Figure C-17. Notice that the Fresh Ideas layer styles are listed in detail under the Effects bar.

7. Click File on the menu bar, then click Save

Modifying type orientation

You can change type orientation (vertical or horizontal) on a layer using the Layer menu. You can click the type layer that you want to change, click Layer on the menu bar, point to Type, then click either Vertical or Horizontal. You can create vertically oriented type by clicking the Type Tool T, then clicking the **Vertically orient text button** T on the tools **option bar**.

FIGURE C-15: Layer Style dialog box

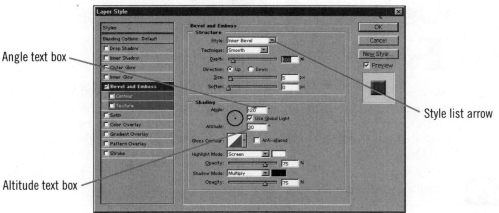

Angle text box

Style list arrow

Altitude text box

FIGURE C-16: Settings in Layer Style dialog box

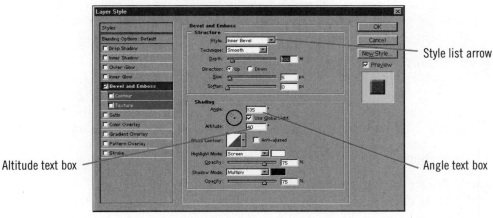

Style list arrow

Altitude text box

Angle text box

FIGURE C-17: Bevel and Emboss style applied to image

Bevel style applied to layer

Layer styles listed under Effects bar

Photoshop 6.0

Using Filters with Type

Like images, filters can be applied to type layers to achieve special effects. Some filter dialog boxes have preview windows that let you see the results of a particular filter before it is applied to the layer. Other filters must be applied to the layer before you can see the results. Before a filter can be applied to a type layer, the type layer must be **rasterized**, or converted to an image layer. Once rasterized, the type cannot be edited because it is composed of pixels. When a type layer is rasterized, the Type layer T and Effects ▶ ● icons disappear from the Layers palette. Erin explains to the interns how filters can be used with type.

Create special text effects

Filters enable you to apply a variety of special effects to type as shown in Figure C-18. Notice that none of the layers in the Layers palette displays the Type layer button T because they have all been rasterized. Once a type layer is rasterized, you cannot edit the type, even if you have not yet applied a filter.

Produce text distortions

Distort filters let you create waves or curves in type. Some of the distortions you can produce include Glass, Pinch, Ripple, Shear, Spherize, Twirl, Wave, and Zigzag. These effects are sometimes used as the basis of a corporate logo. The Twirl dialog box, shown in Figure C-19, lets you determine the amount of twirl effect you want to apply. By dragging the Angle slider, you control how much twirl effect is added to a layer. Most filter dialog boxes have zoom in and zoom out buttons that make it easy to see the effects of the filter.

Create patterns and relief

Many filters let you create the appearance of patterns and relief (the height of ridges within an object). One of the Stylize filters, Wind, applies lines throughout the type, making it appear shredded. The Wind dialog box, shown in Figure C-20, lets you determine the kind of wind and its direction. The Texturizer filter lets you choose the type of texture you want to apply to a layer: Brick, Burlap, Canvas, or Sandstone.

FIGURE C-18: Sample filters applied to type

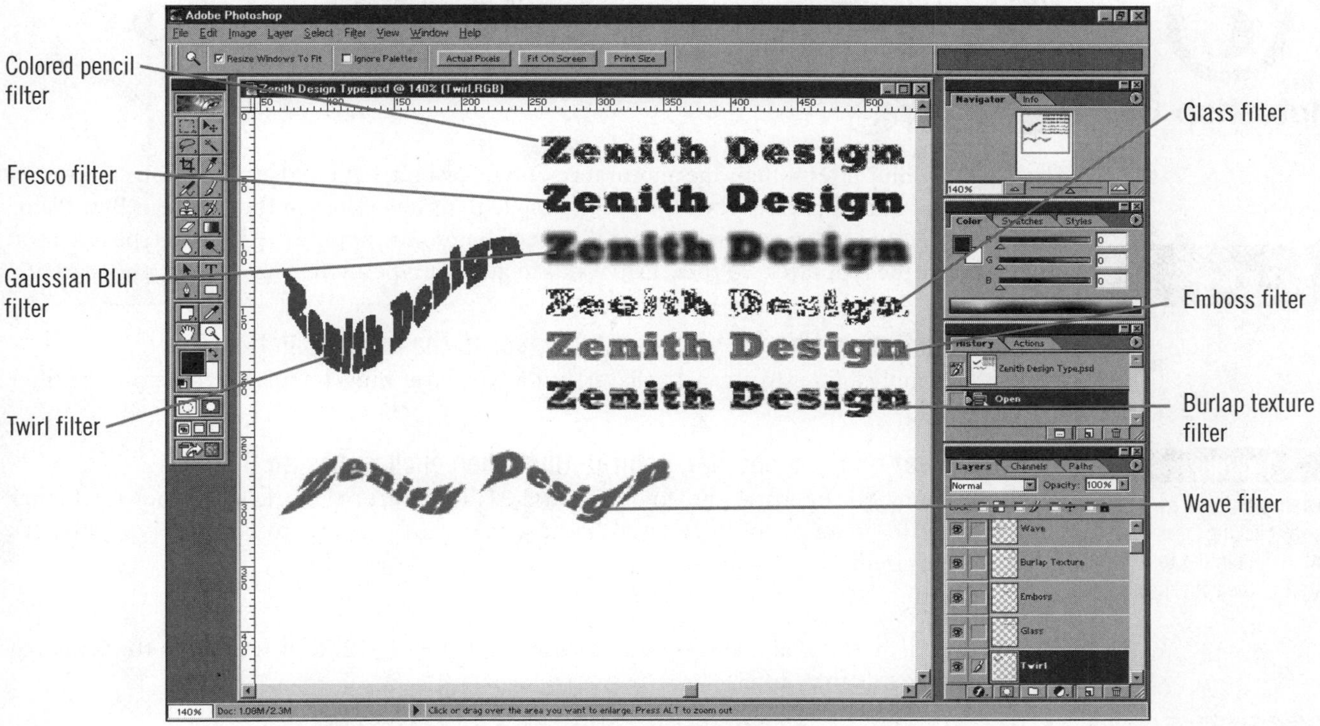

Colored pencil filter

Fresco filter

Gaussian Blur filter

Twirl filter

Glass filter

Emboss filter

Burlap texture filter

Wave filter

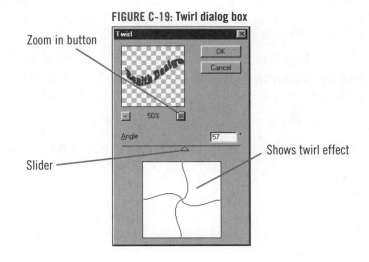

FIGURE C-19: Twirl dialog box

Zoom in button

Slider

Shows twirl effect

FIGURE C-20: Wind dialog box

Zoom out button

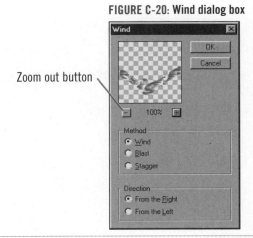

Photoshop 6.0

Photoshop 6.0

Applying a Filter to Type

The Gaussian Blur filter softens the appearance of type by blurring its edge pixels. You can control the amount of blur applied to the type by entering high or low values in the Gaussian Blur dialog box. The higher the blur value, the blurrier the effect. Before you apply any filter to a type layer, you must rasterize the type layer. ✎ Erin wants to give her type a softer, less intrusive appearance.

1. Click the **Decorating for your lifestyle layer** in the Layers palette
You can apply a filter to any active layer, but a type layer must be rasterized before the filter is applied.

Trouble?

You can also rasterize a type layer by clicking Layer on the menu bar, pointing to Rasterize, then clicking Type.

2. Click **Filter** on the menu bar, point to **Blur**, then click **Gaussian Blur**
The warning box opens, as shown in Figure C-21. This warning box lets you choose whether you want to rasterize the type layer, because you won't be able to edit the type after it's been rasterized.

3. Click **OK**
The Gaussian Blur dialog box opens, as shown in Figure C-22. Your settings in the Gaussian Blur dialog box may differ.

Trouble?

Too much blur applied to type can make it unreadable, or cause it to disappear entirely.

4. Drag the **slider** until **0.8** appears in the Radius text box, then click **OK**
Compare your image to Figure C-23. Notice that while the label Effects exists on the Decorating for your lifestyle layer, the **T** no longer appears in the thumbnail area. This is no longer a type layer.

5. Click the **Type Tool** on the toolbox, click the image at **50 H/590 V**, change the **Set the font size list arrow** to **12**, type your name, then click the **Move Tool**
Your name appears in the lower-left corner of the document.

6. Click **File** on the menu bar, then click **Save**

7. Click **File** on the menu bar, click **Print**, then click **OK**

8. **Exit (Win)** or **Quit (Mac)** Photoshop

FIGURE C-21: Warning box

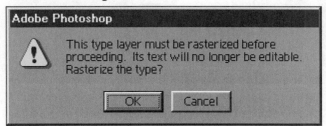

FIGURE C-22: Gaussian Blur dialog box

Slider

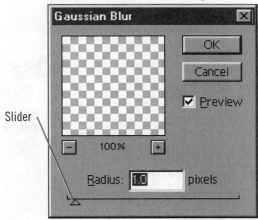

FIGURE C-23: Type with Gaussian Blur filter

No longer a type layer

► Concepts Review

Label each element in the Photoshop window shown in Figure C-24.

FIGURE C-24

Match each button, tool, or pointer with the statement that describes its function.

7. Indicates a type layer   a. IT

8. Aligns type   b. ◯

9. Creates vertical type   c. ⫯

10. Type pointer   d. 🖑

11. Selects color from Color Picker dialog box   e. ☰

12. Deletes state from History palette   f. T

Select the best answer from the list of choices.

13. **Which menu is used to apply styles to type?**
    a. Edit
    b. Image
    c. Layer
    d. Filter

14. **Which button is used to add a layer style to a type layer?**
    a. ▷ 🌑
    b. ▶ 🌑
    c. T
    d. 🌑

15. **Which tool is used to create a horizontal type layer?**
    a. 🖊
    b. IT
    c. T
    d. T

16. **Which pointer is used to sample a color or make a selection from the Swatches palette?**
    a. 🖌
    b. 🖋
    c. ✳
    d. ⬡

17. **Which menu is used to apply a filter?**
    a. Edit
    b. Image
    c. Filter
    d. Window

18. **The process of turning a type layer into a regular layer is called**
    a. Converting.
    b. Rasterizing.
    c. Transforming.
    d. Regulating.

19. **The feature that produces sharp-edged type is called**
    a. Pro-aliasing.
    b. Anti-aliasing.
    c. Anti-jag.
    d. Smoothing.

20. **You can adjust the distance that a character appears from its original position by controlling the**
    a. Baseline.
    b. Home position.
    c. Font shift.
    d. Baseline shift.

21. **The process of adjusting the space between characters is called**
    a. Leading.
    b. Carting.
    c. Kerning.
    d. Leavening.

 Skills Review

1. **Create type.**
    a. Start Photoshop.
    b. Open PS C-2, then save it as *ZD-Logo*.
    c. Make sure the rulers appear.
    d. Use the Type Tool to create a type layer at 25 H and 95 V.
    e. Use the Matisse ITC font. (If necessary, substitute another font.)
    f. Type **Zenith**.
    g. Save your work.

2. **Modify type.**
    a. Use the Type Tool to create a new type layer at 190 H and 95 V.
    b. Type **Design**.
    c. Select the *Design* text.
    d. Change the text color to the color used in the lower-left background. (*Hint*: Use the Eyedropper Tool.)
    e. Save your work.

3. **Create a drop shadow.**
    a. Activate the Zenith layer.
    b. Open the Layer Style dialog box and choose the Drop Shadow style.
    c. If necessary, set the angle to 150°.
    d. Close the Layer Style dialog box.
    e. Save your work.

4. **Change a font and apply anti-aliasing.**
    a. Double-click the Type layer button on the Zenith layer to highlight the Zenith text, then change the type to a 35-point Lucida Sans font. (If necessary, substitute another font.)
    b. Change the Anti-Alias setting to Crisp.
    c. Select the Design type layer text, then change the type to a 35-point Lucida Sans font. (If necessary, substitute another font.)
    d. Save your work.

5. **Apply a Bevel and Emboss style.**
    a. With the Design layer still active, open the Layer Style dialog box for the Bevel and Emboss style.
    b. Set the style to Inner Bevel.
    c. Set the angle to 150 and the altitude to 5°.
    d. Open the Layer Style dialog box for the Bevel and Emboss style for the Zenith type layer.
    e. Set the style to Inner Bevel.
    f. Set the angle to 150 and the altitude to 5°.
    g. Close the Layer Style dialog box.
    h. Save your work.

6. Apply a filter to type.

a. Create a new type layer at 50 H and 125 V.

b. Use a 14-point Lucida Sans font in light blue. (If necessary, substitute another font.)

c. Type your name.

d. Apply a 1.0 pixel Gaussian Blur effect, rasterizing the layer when necessary.

e. Move the Your name layer to the upper-right corner of the image.

f. Save your work.

g. Exit (Win) or Quit (Mac) Photoshop.

▶ Independent Challenges

1. A local flower shop, Beautiful Blooms, asks you to design its color advertisement for the trade magazine *Florists United*. You already started on the image, and need to add some type.

a. Open PS C-3, then save it as *Beautiful Blooms Ad*.

b. Click the Type Tool, then type **Beautiful Blooms**. Choose any font.

c. Create a catchy phrase using the same font as in the previous step, but in a smaller point size.

d. Apply a Drop Shadow style to the name of the floral shop.

e. Apply a Bevel and Emboss style to the catch phrase.

f. Type your name in the lower-left corner of the document.

g. Save and print the document.

2. Your design firm is asked to design an advertisement for a new local organic grocer. The owners also need your help choosing the store's name. Develop an image for the grocery store, and an ad that reflects this image.

a. Create a Photoshop document with the dimensions 360 pixels × 360 pixels, then save it as *Organic Grocer Ad*. (*Hint:* Click the width and height list arrows in the Preferences dialog box to select pixels as your unit of measure.)

b. Using the Type Tool, create a name for the new business. Choose any font and font color.

c. Add another type layer that contains the phrase "Health and Goodness." Use a different font and smaller point size than in the previous step.

d. Apply a Drop Shadow style to the store name.

e. Apply a Bevel and Emboss style to the phrase.

f. If you choose, you can add any colors to the Background layer.

g. Type your name in the lower-left corner of the document.

h. Save and print the document.

3. You are asked to develop text for a new women's perfume. To accomplish this, you want to see samples of other perfume ads.

   a. Obtain at least one color print perfume ad and scan the image. Use the type in the ad to create your own perfume ad.

b. Create a Photoshop document with the dimensions 360 pixels × 360 pixels, then save it as *Perfume Ad*.

c. Add a type layer that contains a name for the new perfume. (You make up the name of the scent.) Choose any font.

d. Add another type layer that contains a catchy phrase that will be used throughout the campaign. Use a different font and smaller point size than in the previous step.

e. Apply styles to each type layer to make the type stand out.

f. Rasterize the perfume name layer and apply a filter to it.

g. If you want, add colors to the Background layer.

h. Type your name in the lower-left corner of the document.

i. Save and print the document.

4. A local computer store, Mega-Bytes, is expanding and has hired you to create a logo using type.

a. Connect to the Internet and go to the following Web sites at:
http://www.course.com
http://www.carlsjr.com
http://www.levenger.com
http://www.lexus.com
http://www.vignette.com

b. Print examples from these links that illustrate logos featuring type.

c. Create a Photoshop document with the dimensions 360 pixels × 280 pixels, then save it as *Mega-Bytes*.

d. Create a layer with type for the company name.

e. Modify the background to make it more appealing, if necessary.

f. Apply your choice of filter to the type.

g. Type your name in the lower-right corner of the document.

h. Save and print this document.

▶ Visual Workshop

Open PS C-4 from the drive and folder where your Project Files are stored and save it as *Spilled Milk*. Use the skills you learned in this unit to modify the image so it looks like Figure C-25. Use the Eyedropper Tool to sample the color for the type layers at 40 H/150 V. Use the 60-point Times New Roman font for the Don't Cry type layer. Create a Bevel and Emboss style on the Don't Cry type layer using the following settings: Angle=100 and Altitude=7°. Type your name in the upper-right corner of the document. Print one copy of the document.

FIGURE C-25

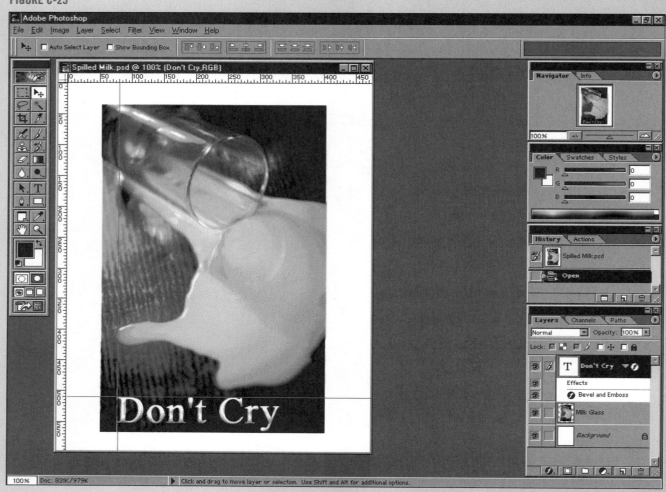

Understanding
Layers

Objectives

► **Define layers**
► **Turn a layer into a background**
► **Add and delete layers**
► **Drag a selection onto a layer**
► **Display and hide layers**
► **Adjust opacity**
► **Stack layers**
► **Flatten layers**

You can create sophisticated images with Photoshop, using multiple layers. You can have a maximum of 8000 layers in each Photoshop document, each containing as much or as little detail as you deem necessary. By placing images and type on separate layers, you can modify them individually. As you add and delete layers, you can hide and display each layer, or change its transparency. The number of layers, and the order in which they are arranged, allow you to continuously change your document's overall appearance, until you get just the look you want. Once your document is finished, you can dramatically reduce its file size by combining all the layers. ✎ Lawrence Catron is an Account Representative at Zenith Design. He is working on a new cover for the New England Bureau of Tourism's fall vacation guide. The cover contains type and image layers that Lawrence needs to rearrange.

Defining Layers

Photoshop 6.0

Layers in a Photoshop image are equivalent to individual clear sheets of plastic that form a stack. Each object created in Photoshop exists on its own individual layer, making it easy to control the position of each layer in the "stack." The advantage to using multiple layers is that you can isolate effects on one layer without affecting the others. The disadvantage of using multiple layers is that your file size may become very large. Before he begins, Lawrence reviews the operation of Photoshop layers.

Details

QuickTip

If a layer name is too long to show in the palette, an ellipsis appears indicating that part of the name is hidden from view. To view the entire name, hold 🖑 over the name in the Layers palette.

The Layers palette

The **Layers palette** lists all the layers within a Photoshop file. By default, this palette is located in the lower-right corner of the screen, but can be moved to a new location by dragging the palette name tab. The **thumbnail**, which appears to the left of the layer name, contains a miniature picture of the layer's content, and may be turned on or off. In some cases, as shown in Figure D-1, the entire name of the layer may not appear in the palette. You can also add color to the area to the left of the thumbnail on each layer. This feature lets you identify layers by flagging them with colors.

Information in the Layers palette

The Layers palette includes several types of layers: background, type, and image (non-type). The Background layer—whose name appears in italics—is always at the bottom of the stack. Type layers contain the Type layer button T , and image layers display their contents in the Layer thumbnail. To make changes to a layer, you must first select it to make it the active layer. As shown in Figure D-1, *Gourds* is the active layer. Active layers are highlighted, and there can only be one active layer at a time. You can hide a layer by clicking the eye button 👁 , and you can display a hidden layer by clicking the Show/Hide layer button ▢ .

QuickTip

You can also drag and drop objects created by other Adobe products, such as Illustrator and InDesign onto a Photoshop document.

Combine images from other files

You can add, delete, and move layers in your document, as necessary. You can also drag a selection from a layer in one Photoshop document onto a new layer in another Photoshop document.

Organize layers

One of the benefits of using layers is that you can rearrange them to create different effects. Figure D-2 contains the same layers as Figure D-1, but they have been arranged differently. Notice that the gourds are partially obscured by the wreath. Dragging the Gourds layer beneath the Wreath layer in the Layers palette created this effect.

Reduce file size

Once you modify the layers, you can flatten them. **Flattening layers** merges all of the visible layers into one layer, and deletes all of the hidden layers, greatly reducing the size of your file. The status bar, as shown in Figure D-2, displays the document's current size and the size it will be when flattened. If you work on a Macintosh, you'll find this information in the lower-left corner of the document window.

FIGURE D-1: Image with multiple layers

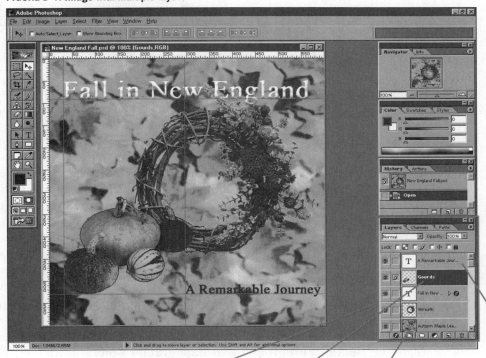

Layers palette   Active layer   Thumbnail

Entire layer
may not be
visible

FIGURE D-2: Layers rearranged

Order of layers
changed

Gourds are
obscured by
the wreath

Wreath layer

Flattened size   Current size   Gourds layer

Photoshop 6.0

Turning a Layer into a Background

The Background layer of any document is the initial layer, and is always located at the bottom of the stack. Its position in the stack cannot be changed, nor can you make alterations to this layer as you would other layers. Background layers can be converted into image layers (non-type layers), and image layers can be converted into background layers. You may want to convert a background layer into an image layer so that you can use the full range of editing tools on the layer content. You may find it necessary to change an image layer into a background layer to ensure that your changes are preserved, and to position the layer at the bottom of the stack. A background layer cannot be modified as extensively as an image layer, so make all your changes to the image layer *before* converting it to a background layer. Lawrence is working on a document that he will use for the cover of his client's travel magazine, *Fall in New England*. Because he has made the necessary changes to the Autumn Maple Leaves layer, he will convert it to a background layer to position the layer at the bottom of the stack, and ensure that the changes are preserved.

Steps

1. Start Photoshop, **Open PS D-1** from the drive and folder where your Project Files are stored, then save it as **New England Fall**

2. Click the **Default Foreground and Background Colors button** on the toolbox, click **View** on the menu bar, then click **Show Rulers** if your rulers are not visible
   The foreground and background colors now display the default settings.

3. Click the **Background layer** in the Layers palette, click the **Delete layer button** in the Layers palette, then click **Yes** in the warning box, as shown in Figure D-3
   Before you can convert an image layer to a background layer, the existing Background layer must be deleted. The Autumn Maple Leaves layer is now the active layer, and the original Background layer is gone, as shown in Figure D-4. You can turn an image layer into a background layer using the Layer menu.

4. Click **Layer** on the menu bar, point to **New**, then click **Background From Layer**
   The Autumn Maple Leaves layer is now the Background layer, as shown in Figure D-5.

5. Click **File** on the menu bar, then click **Save**

Cropping an image

You may want to use an image that, except for a particular portion, is perfect. You can exclude, or **crop**, certain parts of an image using the Crop Tool on the toolbox. Cropping hides areas of an image from view *without* losing resolution quality. To crop an image, click on the toolbox, drag around the area you *want to keep*, then press [Enter] (Win) or [Return] (Mac).

FIGURE D-3: Warning box

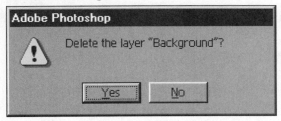

FIGURE D-4: Background layer deleted

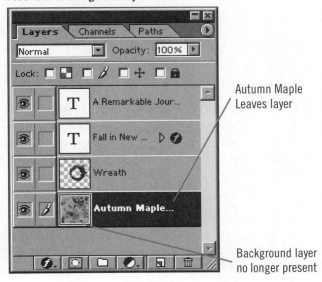

Autumn Maple
Leaves layer

Background layer
no longer present

FIGURE D-5: New Background layer in document

New Background layer

Photoshop 6.0

Adding and Deleting Layers

You can add and delete layers using the Layer menu, the Layers palette menu, or the Create a new layer button in the Layers palette. Photoshop automatically assigns a sequential number to each new layer name, but you can rename a layer at any time. Objects on new layers have a default opacity setting of 100%, which means that objects on lower layers are not visible, and their default blending mode is set to Normal. Lawrence wants to add a new layer to his document so that he can add new imagery to the magazine cover.

Steps

1. Click the **Fall in New England layer** in the Layers palette
   The type layer is active.

QuickTip

You can rename a layer by clicking the Layers palette list arrow ▶, clicking Layer Properties on the Layer palette menu, typing the new name in the Layer Properties dialog box, then clicking OK.

2. Click **Layer** on the menu bar, point to **New**, then click **Layer**
   The New Layer dialog box opens, as shown in Figure D-6. Notice that the default name in the Name text box is Layer 1. Photoshop names this "Layer 1" because the previous layers are not numbered. You can change the layer name in the New Layer dialog box before it appears in the Layers palette.

3. Click **OK**
   The dialog box closes, the new layer, Layer 1, appears above the Fall in New England layer in the Layers palette, and the History palette records the addition of a new layer, as shown in Figure D-7. You can delete a layer before you perform a new task by using the Undo command on the Edit menu, or by using the History palette.

QuickTip

You can also delete a layer by clicking the layer you want to delete, clicking the Layers palette list arrow ▶, then clicking Delete Layer; or by highlighting the layer, clicking the Delete layer button in the Layers palette, then clicking Yes in the warning box.

4. Position 🖑 over **New Layer** in the History palette, then drag 🖑 to the **Delete current state button** 🗑
   The layer is deleted from the Layers palette and the New Layer state is deleted from the History palette. The Background layer, which was the active layer before the new layer was added, is once again active.

5. Click the **Fall in New England layer** in the Layers palette, then click the **Create a new layer button** 🔲 on the Layers palette
   A new layer, Layer 1, appears in the Layers palette, as shown in Figure D-8. When you create a layer using the Create a new layer button, the layer is added with the default settings: Normal mode and 100% opacity.

6. Click **File** on the menu bar, then click **Save**

Merging layers

Merging layers is the process of combining multiple image layers into one layer. Merging layers is useful when you want to make specific edits permanent. In order for layers to be merged, they must be visible and contiguous, meaning that they are next to each other in the Layers palette. You can merge all visible layers within an image, or just a few. Type layers cannot be merged until they are rasterized. To merge two layers, make sure they are contiguous, and that the eye button 👁 is visible on each layer, then click the layer in the higher position in the Layers palette. Click Layer on the menu bar, then click Merge Down. The active layer and the layer immediately beneath it will be combined into a single layer. To merge all visible layers, click the Layers palette list arrow ▶, then click Merge Visible.

FIGURE D-6: New Layer dialog box

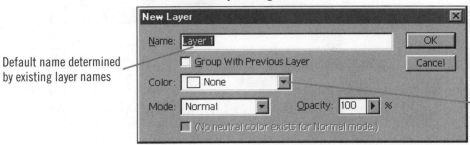

Default name determined
by existing layer names

Click list arrow to add color
to the thumbnail area

FIGURE D-7: New layer in Layers palette

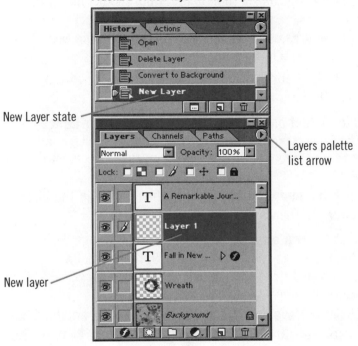

New Layer state

Layers palette
list arrow

New layer

FIGURE D-8: New layer with default settings

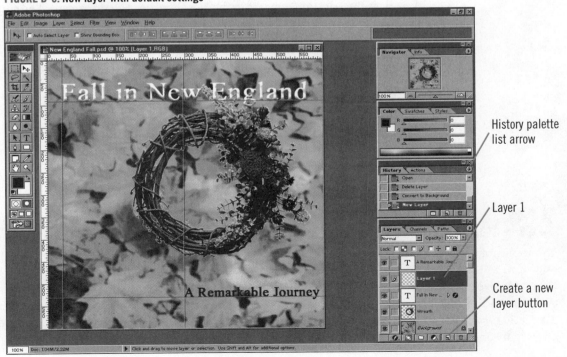

History palette
list arrow

Layer 1

Create a new
layer button

Photoshop 6.0

Dragging a Selection onto a Layer

Photoshop 6.0

In addition to creating images and type within a document, you can incorporate imagery from other documents. You can select an image, or part of an image, from another document, then drag the selection into your open document. A **selection** is an area of an image surrounded by a **marquee**: a dashed line that surrounds the area you want to edit, or move to another document. There are four marquee tools you can use to make selections in Photoshop. Lawrence wants to drag a picture of some gourds from another file into his open document.

Steps

1. Open **Gourds.psd** from the drive and folder where your Project Files are stored
   The document opens in the work area.

2. Click the **Gourds.psd title bar**, then drag it to the right of the New England Fall window so that you can see both documents

3. Click **Select** on the menu bar, then click **Color Range**
   The Color Range dialog box opens. Since the background of the new file is white, and you want to select everything in the document that is *not white*, you can select the white background, and then *invert* the selection.

   QuickTip
   When more than one file is open, each document has its own set of rulers.

4. Click the **Image option button**, then type **0** in the **Fuzziness text box** (or drag the slider) all the way to the left until you see 0

5. Click the **white background** in the Color Range dialog box with 🖊, click the **Invert check box**, as shown in Figure D-9, then click **OK**
   The selected area—everything but the white background—is surrounded by a marquee, as shown in Figure D-10.

6. Click the **Move Tool** ▸⊹ on the toolbox, press and hold **[Alt] (Win)** or **[Option] (Mac)**, position ▸⊹ anywhere over the selection, drag ▸ to the New England Fall document, then release **[Alt] (Win)** or **[Option] (Mac)**
   A copy of the selection appears in the New England Fall document. The gourds were placed on Layer 1, the new layer previously created.

7. Click ▸⊹, if necessary, then drag the **gourds** to the location shown in Figure D-11

8. Click **Edit** on the menu bar, click **Stroke**, type **1** in the Width text box, click the **Inside option button**, then click **OK**
   A thin black outline appears around the gourds. Compare your image to Figure D-11.

9. Click **File** on the menu bar, click **Save**, then close **Gourds.psd**
   The Gourds.psd file closes and the New England Fall document remains open.

Making a selection

You can use a variety of methods and tools to make a selection. You can select a specific part of a layer, or the entire layer. You use selections to isolate the area you want to alter. For example, you can use the Magnetic Lasso Tool 🔲 to select complex shapes by clicking the starting point, tracing an approximate outline, then double-clicking the ending point. Later you can use the Crop Tool 🔲 to trim areas from a selection. Table D-1 shows some of the Photoshop tools you can use to make selections. You can set options for each tool when the tool is active on the tool options bar.

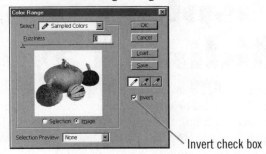

Invert check box

FIGURE D-10: Marquee surrounding selection

Move Tool

Marquee surrounds selection

FIGURE D-11: Selection in image

TABLE D-1: Commonly used selection tools

tool	tool name	tool	tool name
	Rectangular Marquee Tool		Lasso Tool
	Elliptical Marquee Tool		Polygonal Lasso Tool
	Magnetic Lasso Tool		Magic Wand Tool
	Crop Tool		Magic Eraser Tool

Photoshop 6.0

Displaying and Hiding Layers

You can use the Layers palette to control which layers are visible in a document. Only visible layers can be merged or selected. Hiding some layers can make it easier to focus on particular areas of an image. Hiding layers may also improve your computer's performance because memory resources used to display graphics are then made available for other tasks. Lawrence wants to experiment with the effects of displaying and hiding layers.

Steps

1. Verify that **Layer 1** is active

2. Click the **Layers palette list arrow** ◉, then click **Layer Properties**
The Layer Properties dialog box opens, as shown in Figure D-12. You can change the layer name and the layer color in this dialog box.

3. Type **Gourds** in the Name text box, click the **Color list arrow**, click **Yellow**, then click **OK**
The name of the layer changes from Layer 1 to Gourds, and the area to the left of the thumbnail is yellow.

4. Click the **eye button** 👁 on the Gourds layer
The Gourds layer is listed in the Layers palette, but is no longer visible in the document, as shown in Figure D-13.

5. Click 👁 on the A Remarkable Journey layer
The type layer at the bottom of the image is no longer visible. You can hide or display as many layers as you like.

6. Click the **Show/Hide layer button** ▢ on the Gourds layer, then click ▢ on the A Remarkable Journey layer
Both layers are visible again, as shown in Figure D-14.

7. Click **File** on the menu bar, then click **Save**
It is a good idea to save your work early and often in the creation process, especially before making significant changes or printing.

> **QuickTip**
> Only visible layers can be flattened, merged, or printed.

CLUES TO USE

Hiding Layers palette thumbnails

Displaying thumbnails next to layer names in the Layers palette requires computer memory. You can improve your computer's performance by turning off the layer thumbnail display. Smaller files open faster and take up less disk space. Turning thumbnails off also frees up more space in the Layers palette. You can remove layer thumbnails by clicking the Layers palette list arrow ◉, then clicking Palette Options. Click the None option button, then click OK. The thumbnails no longer appear in the Layers palette.

FIGURE D-12: Layer Properties dialog box

Type new layer name here ⟶

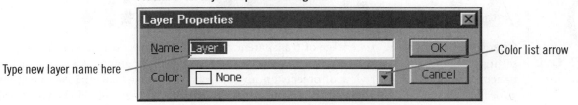

Color list arrow

FIGURE D-13: Gourds layer hidden

Gourds no longer appear ⟶

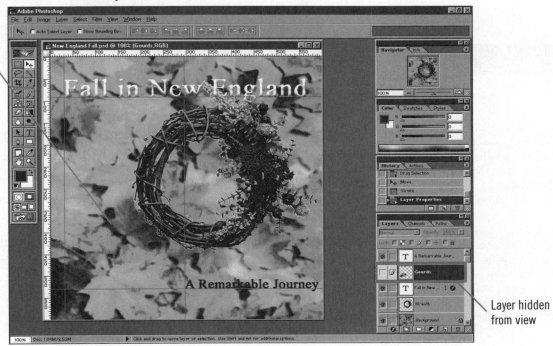

Layer hidden from view

FIGURE D-14: All layers visible

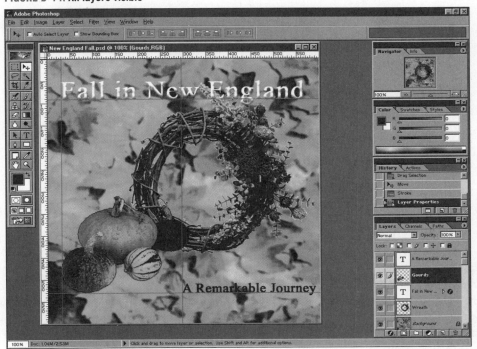

Photoshop 6.0

Adjusting Opacity

Opacity determines the percentage of transparency applied to a layer. You can use the Opacity setting in the Layers palette to control a layer's transparency in a document. A layer with 100% opacity will obstruct your view of objects on lower layers, while a layer with 15% opacity will appear almost invisible. In other words, a low opacity means that more pixels will be visible from the lower layers. You can set opacity by using the Opacity slider in the Layers palette, or by entering a value in the Opacity text box in the Layer Style dialog box. ✏️ Lawrence wants to change the opacity of several layers in the image. He starts with the Wreath layer.

Steps

1. Double-click the **Wreath layer** in the Layers palette
The Layer Style dialog box opens.

You can reposition the Layer Style dialog box if you cannot see the wreath.

2. Type **80** in the Opacity text box, as shown in Figure D-15, then click **OK**
Notice that the wreath appears to blend in more with the background of the leaves.

3. Click the **Gourds layer** in the Layers palette
The opacity information in the Layers palette is located directly beneath the palette tabs. You can change the opacity setting by clicking the Opacity list arrow, which displays the Opacity slider.

You can also change the opacity information by double-clicking the Opacity text box in the Layers palette, and entering a new value.

4. Click the **Opacity list arrow** in the Layers palette, then drag the slider until **85** appears in the Opacity text box
The Gourds layer is subtler and displays a slight tint of the Background layer color. Compare your Layers palette to Figure D-16.

5. Press **[Enter] (Win)** or **[Return] (Mac)**
The slider is no longer visible. Compare your screen to Figure D-17.

6. Click **File** on the menu bar, then click **Save**

Applying transformations

After you transform an image, you can apply the changes by pressing [Enter] (Win) or [Return] (Mac). If you do not press [Enter] (Win) or [Return] (Mac), and attempt to make another modification, the Transforming warning box appears. Click Apply to accept the transformation you made to the layer.

▶ **PHOTOSHOP 84 UNDERSTANDING LAYERS**

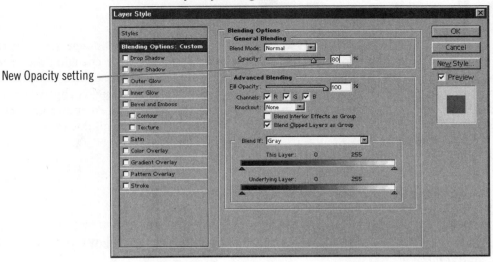

New Opacity setting

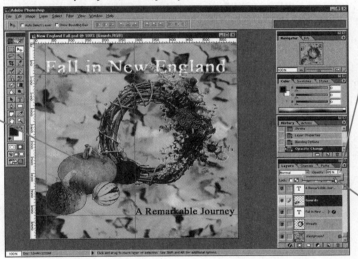

Lower layer color shows through

Click list arrow to display Opacity slider

Drag Opacity slider to change Opacity setting

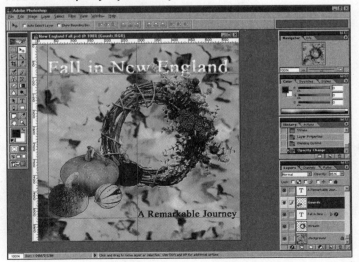

Photoshop 6.0

Stacking Layers

One advantage of working with layers in Photoshop is the flexibility and independence you have to manipulate each layer. For example, you can manipulate layers by changing the order in which they are stacked. You can generate different effects by adjusting the opacity in one or more layers, then changing their position in the Layers palette. You can easily change the stacking order by dragging a layer up or down in the Layers palette. Lawrence wants to change the position of several layers in the stack to view different variations of his document.

Steps

QuickTip

Use 👆 to drag the layer to the exact position you want in the Layers palette.

1. Click the **Wreath layer** in the Layers palette, then drag it **above the Fall in New England layer**
   Figure D-18 shows the layer being dragged to its new position. Some of the text is hidden by the wreath flowers, as shown in Figure D-19.

2. Click the **Gourds layer**, then drag it **beneath the Wreath layer**
   The right portion of the gourds object falls behind the wreath. Figure D-20 shows the effect of moving this layer.

3. Position 🖐 over **the bottom Layer Order state** in the History palette, then drag 👆 to the **Delete current state button** 🗑
   The Layer Order state is deleted from the History palette, and the gourds are completely visible again.

4. Click **File** on the menu bar, then click **Save**

Duplicating a layer

When you add a new layer using the Create a new layer button 🔲 in the Layers palette, it contains default settings. You can also duplicate an existing layer and copy its settings. Duplicating a layer is a good way to preserve the modifications you have made to it. You can then modify the duplicate layer and not worry about losing your original work. Create a duplicate layer by selecting the layer you want to copy, clicking the Layers palette list arrow ▶ to show the Layers palette menu, then clicking Duplicate Layer. The new layer will appear above the original.

FIGURE D-18: Layer being dragged to a new position

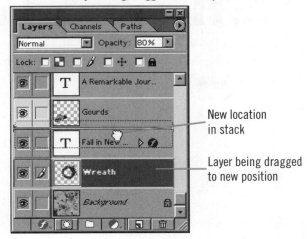

New location
in stack

Layer being dragged
to new position

FIGURE D-19: Effect of rearranging layers

Wreath flowers
hiding text

Type layer is less
visible

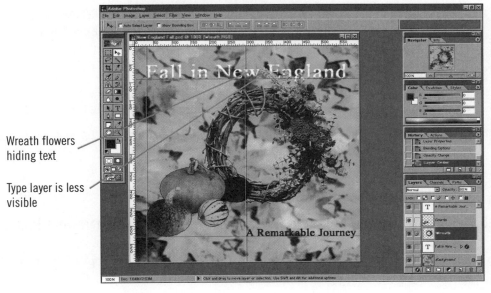

FIGURE D-20: Gourds image behind Wreath layer

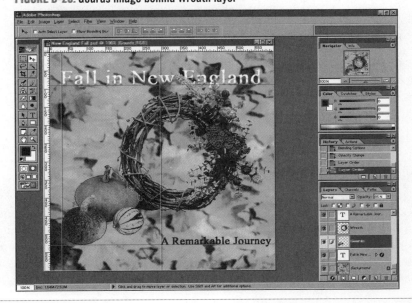

Flattening Layers

Once you make all the necessary modifications to your document, you can greatly reduce the file size by flattening the layers. **Flattening** merges all visible layers into a single background layer. Because flattening removes a document's individual layers, it's a good idea to make a copy of the original document *before* it is flattened. Lawrence wants to save a copy of his image and then flatten it.

Steps

1. Click **File** on the menu bar, then click **Save As**
   The Save As dialog box opens.

2. Click the **Save in list arrow (Win)** or the **Current file location list arrow (Mac)** to find the drive and folder where you store your Project Files, then click the **As a Copy check box**
   "Copy" is added after the existing filename, as shown in Figure D-21.

3. Click **Save**
   The Save As dialog box closes, the New England Fall copy document is stored with your Project Files, and the New England Fall document remains open, ready to be flattened.

4. Click the **Type Tool** T on the toolbox, then type your name in the lower-left corner of the document, then click the Move Tool

5. Click **Layer** on the menu bar, then click **Flatten Image**
   The document has one Background layer.

6. **Open New England Fall copy** from the drive and folder where your Project Files are stored
   The copy opens on top of the flattened document. Notice that the copy of the document still has five layers in the Layers palette.

7. Click **Window** on the menu bar, then click **New England Fall.psd** *(at the bottom of the list)*
   The flattened document opens on top of the copy, as shown in Figure D-22. The flattened copy has only one layer, the Background layer.

8. Click **File** on the menu bar, click **Save**, click **File** on the menu bar, then click **Print**

9. **Exit (Win)** or **Quit (Mac)** Photoshop

Merging versus flattening

Flattening is the process of combining all visible layers into a single layer. *It should be the last step in a project.* Flattening discards all hidden layers, so make sure that all layers meant to be seen are visible before the document is flattened. Use the Merge command when you want to combine several—but not all—displayed layers. Flatten an image when your project is complete, and you want to compact the layers and reduce the file size. Make sure that the eye button is visible for all the layers you want to merge, and that a visible layer is active. Click the Layers palette list arrow, then click Merge Visible.

FIGURE D-21: Save As dialog box

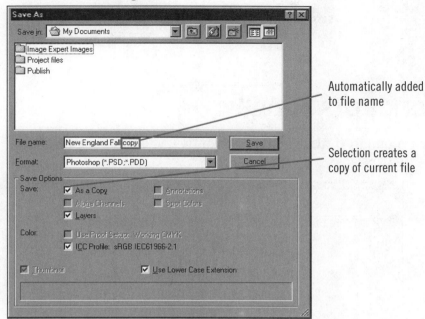

Automatically added to file name

Selection creates a copy of current file

FIGURE D-22: Flattened and layered documents

Flattened document

Layered document

Flattened document contains one layer

Photoshop 6.0

Practice

▶ Concepts Review

Label each element in the Photoshop window shown in **Figure D-23.**

FIGURE D-23

Match each term or phrase with the statement that describes its function.

7. **Background layer**
8. **Flattening**
9. **Opacity**
10. **Layer properties dialog box**
11. **Merge**
12. **Selection marquee**

a. Compacts layers into a single layer
b. Names a layer
c. Combines one layer with the layer beneath it
d. Dashed line surrounding an area
e. Amount of transparency
f. Written in italics

Select the best answer from the list of choices.

13. Which menu do you use to flatten a document?
  a. File
  b. Edit
  c. Image
  d. Layer

14. Which button do you click to modify options for the Layers palette?
  a.
  b.
  c.
  d.

15. Which tool do you use to create a marquee?
  a.
  b.
  c.
  d.

16. Which pointer do you use to define a selection?
  a.
  b.
  c.
  d.

17. Which statement is incorrect?
  a. Only visible layers can be merged.
  b. Only visible layers can be merged or selected.
  c. Only visible layers can be selected.
  d. Only invisible layers can be merged or selected.

18. Which button do you click to hide a layer?
  a.
  b.
  c.
  d.

19. Which of the following is *not* true about flattening?
  a. It makes the file size smaller.
  b. It condenses the layers into a single layer.
  c. It discards all hidden layers.
  d. It makes the file size larger.

20. **The percentage of transparency in each layer is called**
    a. Transparency.
    b. Sheerness.
    c. Quality.
    d. None of the above

21. **Which palette do you use to undo Photoshop tasks?**
    a. Layers
    b. Undo
    c. Edit
    d. History

▶ Skills Review

1. **Turn a layer into a background.**
   a. Start Photoshop.
   b. Open PS D-2 from the drive and folder where your Project Files are stored, then save it as *Music World*.
   c. Make sure the rulers appear with pixels.
   d. Make the Background layer active.
   e. Delete the Background layer.
   f. Verify that the Brown blend layer is active, click Layer on the menu bar, point to New, then click Background From Layer.
   g. Save your work.

2. **Add and delete layers.**
   a. Make Layer 2 active.
   b. Click Layer on the menu bar, point to New, then click Layer.
   c. Accept the default name (Layer 4).
   d. Change the color of the thumbnail to Orange, then click OK.
   e. Drag the New Layer state in the History palette to the Delete current state button.
   f. Make Layer 2 active, then click the Create a new layer button in the Layers palette.
   g. Save your work.

3. **Drag a selection onto a layer.**
   a. Open Horn.psd from the drive and folder where your Project Files are stored.
   b. Click the Horn.psd title bar, then drag it to the right of the Music World document.
   c. Click Select on the menu bar, then click Color Range.
   d. Verify that the Image option button is selected, and that Fuzziness is set to 0.
   e. Click anywhere on the white background, click the Invert check box, then click OK.
   f. Click the Move Tool, click the selection, press and hold [Alt] (Win) or [Option] (Mac), then drag the selection into the Music World document.
   g. Drag the horn so that the upper-left edge of the instrument is at approximately 0 H/10 V.
   h. Save your work.

4. **Adjust opacity.**
   a. Drag Layer 4 above Layer 3.
   b. Use the Layers palette menu to change the name of Layer 4 to *Horn*.
   c. Change the opacity for the Horn layer to 55%.
   d. Save your work.

5. **Stack layers.**
   a. Drag the Horn layer so it is beneath Layer 2.
   b. Hide Layer 1.
   c. Save your work.

6. **Flatten layers.**
   a. Double-click the Type layer button on the Name layer.
   b. Select the existing text, type your name, then click the Move Tool.
   c. Save your work.
   d. Click File on the menu bar, then click Save As.
   e. Click the As a Copy check box, then click Save.
   f. Click Layer on the menu bar, then click Flatten Image (*Hint*: Be sure to discard hidden layers).
   g. Save your work.
   h. Print one copy of Music World.
   i. Exit (Win) or Quit (Mac) Photoshop.

▶ Independent Challenges

1. One of the gorillas in your local zoo is pregnant. The zoo hires you to create a promotional billboard commemorating this event for the upcoming season. The Board of Directors decides that the billboard should be humorous.

a. Create a Photoshop document with the dimensions 300 pixels × 300 pixels and save it as *Zoo Billboard*.
b. Create a new layer in the Layers palette.
c. Open Gorilla.psd from the drive and folder where your Project Files are stored.
d. Use any selection method to create a marquee around the gorilla, then drag the selection onto the new layer in the Zoo Billboard document.
e. Change the opacity of the layer containing the gorilla.
f. Create any type layers you feel add humor to the image.
g. Apply desired type effects.
h. Type your name in the lower-left corner of the document.
i. Save and print the document.

2. The Albuquerque International Balloon Fiesta is preparing for next season, and hires you to design a new advertisement for international promotions.

    a. Create a Photoshop document with the dimensions 360 pixels × 360 pixels, then save it as *Balloon Fiesta*.

    b. Create a new layer in the Layers palette.

    c. Open Balloons.psd from the drive and folder where your Project Files are stored.

    d. Use any selection method to create a marquee within the document, then drag the selection onto the new layer in the Balloon Fiesta document.

    e. Create a type layer and add a caption to the image.

    f. Apply desired type effects.

    g. Change the opacity of the layer containing the balloons.

    h. Save a copy of the document using Photoshop's default naming convention.

    i. Type your name in the upper-left corner of the document.

    j. Flatten the Balloon Fiesta document.

    k. Save and print the document.

3. Literacy is an important issue to your community. Your local education board asks you to create an ad that promotes the importance of literacy.

    a. Locate a color print ad about reading or education. Scan the image and save it in the drive and folder where your Project Files are stored.

    b. Create a Photoshop document with the dimensions 360 pixels × 360 pixels, then save it as *Literacy Promotion*.

    c. Create a new layer.

    d. Use any selection tool to create a selection within the scanned image, then drag the selection onto the new layer in the Literacy Promotion document.

    e. Add any type layers that enhance the image.

    f. Apply desired type effects.

    g. Change the opacity of one layer.

    h. Save a copy of the document using Photoshop's default naming convention.

    i. Type your name in the lower-right corner of the document.

    j. Flatten the Literacy Promotion document.

    k. Save and print the document.

4. You can use the Web to gain more experience using Photoshop layers. In addition to forums, FAQ pages, and product updates, you can find lessons that show you different ways to use Photoshop.

a. Connect to the Internet and go to Laurie McCanna's Design Pages at *http://www.mccannas. com/pshop/pshop5.htm.* (This tutorial works with Photoshop Versions 3 through 6.)

b. Print the contents of this page.

c. Follow the instructions in this exercise.

d. Create a layer that contains your name.

e. Save and print this document.

► Visual Workshop

Open PS D-3 from the drive and folder where your Project Files are stored, then save it as *Breakfast of Champions*. Use the skills you learned in this unit to modify the file so it looks like Figure D-24. Replace the existing type on the Name layer with your own name. Save your work, save a copy of the file using the default naming scheme, flatten, then print the document. (*Hint*: Discard hidden layers during the flattening process.)

FIGURE D-24

Using
Layers to Finesse a Document

Objectives

- ► **Understand blending modes**
- ► **Create a layer mask**
- ► **Paint a layer mask**
- ► **Link and unlink layers**
- ► **Blend pixels between layers**
- ► **Remove a layer mask**
- ► **Add an adjustment layer**
- ► **Create a clipping group**

Now that you have acquired a basic understanding of Photoshop layers, you are ready to learn about advanced layering techniques. You can change the appearance of individual layers in a document by using blending modes, masks, and adjustment layers. These features let you fine-tune layer settings with dramatic results. Intern Jan Rodgers is working on Zenith Design's latest project: a display ad for Rainbow Fruit & Nuts, a retailer with a storefront and a Web site.

Understanding Blending Modes

Photoshop 6.0

Blending modes, explained below, are used with painting and editing tools to manipulate the appearance of a layer's **base color**, the original color of the image. When a blending mode is applied to a layer, the color applied is called the **blend color**. The color created as a result of applying the blend color is appropriately named the **result color**. Blending modes allow you to control the way layers appear in a document. The default blending mode is called **Normal**, and is also referred to as the **threshold**, or the starting point for applying other blending modes. The active layer, shown in Figure E-1, has the Normal blending mode applied to it. You cannot apply blending modes to the Background layer. Jan reviews the Photoshop blending modes.

QuickTip

In Dissolve blending mode, the lower the opacity, the grainier the image.

QuickTip

Multiplying any color with black produces black. Multiplying any color with white leaves the color unchanged.

QuickTip

The Soft Light blending mode effect is similar to that of a diffused spotlight; the Hard Light blending mode effect is similar to a harsh spotlight.

Dissolve, Behind, and Clear modes
The Dissolve blending mode creates a grainy, mottled appearance. The Behind blending mode paints on the transparent part of the layer. The Clear blend mode paints individual pixels. Both modes are available only when the Lock transparent pixels ▢▢ check box is *not* checked.

Multiply and Screen modes
The Multiply blend mode creates semi-transparent shadow effects. This mode assesses the information in each channel, then multiplies the value of the base color by the blend color. The result color is always *darker* than the base color. The Screen mode multiplies the value of the inverse of the blend and base colors. After it is applied, the result color is always *lighter* than the base color.

Overlay mode
In this mode, dark and light values (luminosity) are preserved, dark base colors are multiplied (darkened), and light areas are screened (lightened).

Soft Light and Hard Light modes
The Soft Light blending mode lightens a light base color and darkens a dark base color. The Hard Light blending mode creates a similar effect, but provides greater contrast between the base and layer colors. The Hard Light blending mode is applied to the active layer in Figure E-2.

Color Dodge and Color Burn modes
The Color Dodge blending mode brightens the base color to reflect the blend color. The Color Burn blending mode darkens the base color to reflect the blend color.

Darken and Lighten modes
The Darken blending mode selects a new result color based on whichever color is darker—the base color or the blend color. The Lighten blending mode selects a new result color based on the lighter of the two colors.

Difference and Exclusion modes
The Difference blending mode subtracts the value of the blend color from the value of the base color, or vice versa, depending on which color has the greater brightness value. The Exclusion blending mode creates an effect similar to the Difference blending mode, but with less contrast between the blend and base colors.

Color and Luminosity modes
The Color blending mode creates a result color with the luminance of the base color, and the hue and saturation of the blend color. The Luminosity blending mode creates a result color with the hue and saturation of the base color, and the luminance of the blend color.

Hue and Saturation modes
The Hue blending mode creates a result color with the luminance of the base color and the hue of the blend color. The Saturation blending mode creates a result color with the luminance of the base color and saturation of the blend color.

FIGURE E-1: Normal blending mode applied to the active layer

Blending mode for active layer

FIGURE E-2: Hard Light blending mode applied to active layer

Hard Light blending mode   Active layer

Photoshop 6.0

Creating a Layer Mask

You can hide or reveal selections within a layer by using a layer mask. A **layer mask** can cover an entire layer or specific areas within a layer. When a layer contains a mask, a Layer mask thumbnail appears in the Layers palette to the left of the layer name. As you hide or reveal portions of a layer, the Layer mask thumbnail mirrors the changes you make to the object. You can use tools on the toolbox to create the areas that will be masked. You can apply a mask to the selection, or you can apply the mask to everything except the selection. ✎ Jan wants to apply oval-shaped masks to the Rainbow and Bananas layers.

Steps

1. Start Photoshop, open **PS E-1** from the drive and folder where your Project Files are stored, then save it as **Rainbow Fruit**

2. Click the **Default Foreground and Background Colors button** 🖫 on the toolbox, click **View** on the menu bar, then click **Show Rulers** if necessary
   The default foreground and background colors appear.

QuickTip

You can alternate between displaying 🔲 and 🔘 as the active marquee tool by clicking the active marquee tool, pressing and holding [Shift], pressing M, then releasing [Shift].

3. Click the **Rainbow layer** in the Layers palette, click the **Marquee Tool** 🔲 on the toolbox, then hold the mouse button until the tools list appears, click the **Elliptical Marquee Tool** 🔘, then drag + from **30 H/20 V to 555 H/540 V** using the snap-to feature of the guides to locate the coordinates
   The elliptical marquee on the Rainbow layer, as shown in Figure E-3, represents the area that remains in view after the mask is added to the layer. You can also control the softness of the selection's edges, or **feathering**, by typing pixel values in the Feather text box on the tool options bar.

QuickTip

You can add an unlimited number of masks to a document, but only one mask to each layer.

4. Click **Layer** on the menu bar, point to **Add Layer Mask**, then click **Reveal Selection**
   The mask leaves the selected area visible, and hides content on the Rainbow layer that was not surrounded by the elliptical marquee selection.

QuickTip

You can deselect a marquee by clicking Select on the menu bar, then clicking Deselect, or by clicking in another area of the image.

5. Click the **Bananas layer** in the Layers palette, drag + from **80 H/210 V to 280 H/360 V**
   An elliptical marquee, known as the active selection, surrounds the bananas, as shown in Figure E-4.

QuickTip

You can press and hold [Alt] (Win) or [Option] (Mac) while clicking 🔳 to add a mask that *hides* the selection.

6. Click the **Add a mask button** 🔳 in the Layers palette
   The mask displays the selected area. Using the Add a mask button in the Layers palette is another way to apply a mask to a layer. The mask surrounds the bananas and partially obscures the layer's lower-left edge. The Rainbow and Bananas layers each contain a Layer mask thumbnail, as shown in Figure E-5. The white area in the Layer mask thumbnail represents the mask applied to the layer.

7. Click **File** on the menu bar, then click **Save**

FIGURE E-3: Elliptical selection on Rainbow layer

Elliptical Marquee Tool

Elliptical selection

FIGURE E-4: Elliptical selection on Bananas layer

Elliptical selection

Layer mask thumbnail on Rainbow layer

Click to create layer mask

FIGURE E-5: Document with layer masks

Layer mask thumbnail on Bananas layer

Photoshop 6.0

Painting a Layer Mask

Once you add a layer mask to a layer, you can reshape it with the Paintbrush Tool and a specific brush size, or tip. When you paint the image with a black foreground, the size of the mask *increases*, and each brush stroke hides pixels on the image layer. When you paint an object using white as the foreground color, the size of the mask *decreases*, and each brush stroke restores pixels of the layer object. The Layer mask thumbnail in the Layers palette automatically updates itself to reflect changes you make to the mask. Jan will use the Paintbrush Tool to paint parts of the mask so she can hide some of the Bananas layer. She begins by zooming in on the area she will paint.

Steps

1. Make sure that the **Bananas layer** is the active layer

2. Click the **Zoom Tool** on the toolbox, make sure the **Resize Windows To Fit check box** on the tool options bar is selected, then click at **150 H/300 V** until the zoom factor is 200%
   The view of the bananas is enlarged, making it easier to see specific areas during the painting process.

QuickTip

The current brush tip size and style shown on the tool options bar is the last tip style that was used.

3. Click the **Paintbrush Tool** on the toolbox, click the **Painting Brush list arrow** on the tool options bar, click the **second brush tip from the left in the second row**, then press **[Enter] (Win)** or **[Return] (Mac)** to close the Brush pop-up palette
   Now you can use the Paintbrush Tool to paint areas on the layer and reshape the mask. The Paintbrush Tool uses the current foreground color.

Trouble?

If the opacity is less than 100%, the painting effects applied to the layer will differ.

4. Verify that the Painting Mode is set to **Normal** and that the Opacity setting is **100%** on the tool options bar, then click the **Layer mask thumbnail** on the Bananas layer
   The mask icon, as shown in Figure E-6, indicates that the next action will affect the mask rather than the layer.

5. Click the **Switch Foreground and Background Colors button** on the toolbox
   The foreground color (for the layer mask) is now black.

Trouble?

If you click the mouse more than once during the painting process, a new state will be created for each mouse click, and your History palette will contain more states than those shown here.

6. Using Figure E-7 as a guide, drag along the **left-most banana**
   As you make changes to the layer mask, the Layer mask thumbnail reflects those changes, and the left-most banana is no longer visible. Now you want to remove the right-most banana.

7. Drag along the right edge of the object, until the **right-most banana** is no longer visible
   Compare your image to Figure E-8. You can use the Brushes pop-up palette to change the size and style of the brush tip, as necessary.

8. Click on the toolbox, press **[Alt] (Win)** or **[Option] (Mac)**, click at **150 H/300 V** until the zoom factor is 100%, then release **[Alt] (Win)** or **[Option] (Mac)**
   The document returns to its original size.

9. Click **File** on the menu bar, then click **Save**

FIGURE E-6: Mask icons in Layers palette

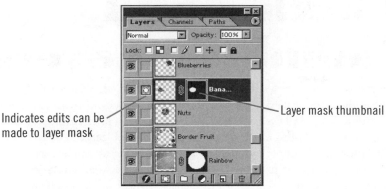

Indicates edits can be made to layer mask

Layer mask thumbnail

FIGURE E-7: Layer mask painted

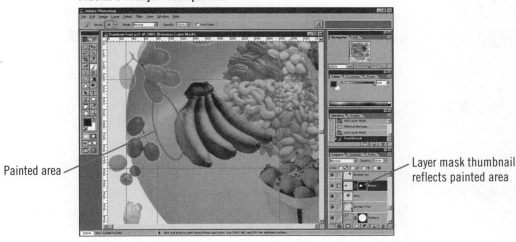

Painted area

Layer mask thumbnail reflects painted area

FIGURE E-8: Modified layer mask

Editing the layer mask versus editing the layer

Normally, when you click a layer, the paintbrush icon appears in the column to the left of the Layer thumbnail. This icon indicates that the changes you make will affect the layer *only*. When you click the Layer mask thumbnail, the mask icon appears.

It indicates that any changes you make to the layer will affect the mask *only*. This column in the Layers palette displays several different icons, including the link icon.

Linking and Unlinking Layers

Additional contents of a layer, such as a mask, are linked to a layer. This means that when you move a layer in the Layers palette, the mask added to that layer moves as well. The link icon 🔗 between the Layer thumbnail and the Layer mask thumbnail on a layer automatically appears and indicates that the layer mask is linked to the layer. Just as multiple objects can be grouped to form a single object in an art program, multiple layers can be linked to move as a single layer in Photoshop. You can link one or more layers to the *active* layer. When the link between layers is no longer necessary, it can be broken, and the layers will return to their individual status—as if you ungrouped grouped objects.
Once Jan makes her modifications to the layers, she wants to link some of the layers, and then move them to a new location in the document.

QuickTip

Linked layers *do not* have to be contiguous (next to each other) in the Layers palette.

QuickTip

The link icon appears in the same column that holds the paintbrush and mask icons.

QuickTip

You can unlink layers by clicking the link icon on the layer you want to exclude from the link.

1. Verify that the **Bananas layer** in the Layers palette is active

2. Click the **empty gray square** ⬜ on the **Nuts layer** in the Layers palette
The link icon 🔗 appears in the column to the left of the Nuts Layer thumbnail.

3. Click ⬜ on the **Blueberries layer** in the Layers palette
The link icon appears in the column to the left of the Blueberries Layer thumbnail. The link icon that appears in the column to the left of the Layer thumbnail indicates the connection. Compare your screen to Figure E-9. The Blueberries layer and the Nuts layer are linked to the Bananas layer. If you drag the blueberries, nuts, or bananas in the document window, all three objects will move together.

4. Click the **link icon** 🔗 on the **Nuts layer** in the Layers palette
The link icon disappears and the Nuts layer is no longer linked to the Bananas layer, or the Blueberries layer.

5. Drag the **Bananas layer** below the **Nuts layer**
The bottom-left edge of the Nuts layer overlaps the Bananas layer. Compare your image to Figure E-10. Moving the linked layers can affect the appearance of other layers in the document.

6. Click **File** on the menu bar, then click **Save**

Link icon

FIGURE E-10: Blueberries layer linked to Bananas layer

Linked to active layer

Transforming linked layers

Linked layers can be transformed using any of the Transform commands under the Edit menu. For example, you may want to scale or rotate layers that were linked together. When you use one of the Transform commands, selection handles, which are dragged to transform the layer, appear in the work area surrounding the contents of the active layer. Layers that are linked to the active layer will be transformed simultaneously and in the same way that the active layer is transformed.

Blending Pixels Between Layers

You can control *which* pixels from the active layer are blended with pixels from layers lower in the stack using the Layer Style dialog box. You can control *how* these pixels are blended by using the This Layer and Underlying Layer sliders. The **This Layer sliders** are used to specify the range of pixels that will be blended on the active layer. The **Underlying Layer sliders** are used to specify the range of pixels that will be blended on lower—but still visible—layers. Both sliders adjust the brightness range of the blended pixels. Jan wants to blend the pixels on the Strawberries layer with the layer below it.

Steps

1. Double-click the **Strawberries layer** in the Layers palette

The Layer Style dialog box opens, as shown in Figure E-11.

QuickTip

Move the Layer Style dialog box if it obscures your view of the strawberries.

2. Verify that the **Preview check box** is selected

As you drag the sliders in this dialog box, the Preview check box allows you to instantly see your changes.

3. Click the **Drop Shadow check box**

A drop shadow is visible in the preview box and on the Strawberries layer. The drop shadow adds depth to the layer contents.

Trouble?

You will not see the Blend If list arrow if the Drop Shadow bar is highlighted in the Layer Style dialog box. Click the Blending Options: Custom bar directly above the Drop Shadow bar to highlight it instead.

4. Click the **Blend If list arrow**, then click **Red**

The Blend If list arrow lets you choose a color range for pixels you want to blend, producing a smooth transition between blended and unblended areas. By selecting Red, you specified that only red pixels will be blended. The This Layer and Underlying Layer sliders display shades of red. You can drag these sliders to further specify the *shades* of red pixels on the Strawberries layer that will be blended with the layer below it.

5. Drag the **right This Layer slider** ▲ to the left until you reach the **220** location, as shown in Figure E-12, then click **OK**

The This Layer slider specifies the active layer's range of pixels that will be blended. Notice that the tops of the strawberries blend into the layer below. Background pixels with values higher than 150 tend to remain unblended and become transparent in the document. Compare your image to Figure E-13.

6. Click **File** on the menu bar, then click **Save**

Using duplicate layers to blend pixels

You can create interesting effects by duplicating layers. To duplicate a layer, click the layer to activate it, click the Layers palette list arrow ⬤, click Duplicate Layer, then click OK. The duplicate layer is given the same name as the active layer with "copy" attached to it.

You can modify the duplicate layer by applying effects or masks to it. In addition, you can alter a document's appearance by moving the original and duplicate layers to different positions in the stack.

FIGURE E-11: Layer Style dialog box

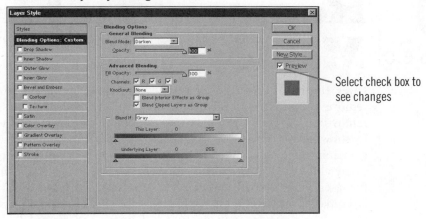

Select check box to see changes

FIGURE E-12: This Layer slider adjusted

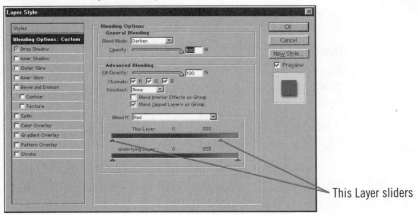

This Layer sliders

FIGURE E-13: Pixels blended in the Strawberries layer

Blended areas

Photoshop 6.0

Removing a Layer Mask

Layer effects can be removed permanently or temporarily. You might want to temporarily remove a layer mask to see how a layer looks *without* the mask. One reason for temporarily removing a layer effect would be to create a duplicate layer, and then apply different effects to it. By showing and hiding the original layer and the duplicate, you can see how the same layer can be manipulated using different masks. When you permanently remove a layer mask, Photoshop asks you if you want to apply the mask to the layer before removing it. If you select this option, the layer will retain the *appearance* of the mask effect, but it will no longer contain the actual layer mask. Each layer mask increases the file size, so you should perform some routine maintenance as you finalize your document. Remove and discard any unnecessary, unwanted layer masks, and apply and discard any necessary, effective layer masks. ✒ Jan wants to experiment with removing layer masks to see how this procedure is accomplished.

Steps

1. **Click the Bananas layer in the Layers palette, click Layer on the menu bar, then click Disable Layer Mask**

   The bananas are no longer masked. A red X appears on the Bananas layer in the Layers palette, as shown in Figure E-14. This icon indicates that the layer mask is still in place, but its effect is not currently visible.

2. **Click Layer on the menu bar, then click Enable Layer Mask**

   The layer mask is restored.

3. **Click the Layer mask thumbnail on the Rainbow layer in the Layers palette**

   The mask icon ▣ appears in the column to the left of the Layer thumbnail, indicating that the next action will affect the mask rather than the layer.

> **QuickTip**
>
> When you remove a layer effect such as a mask, be sure to click the Layer mask thumbnail *before* you perform another action.

4. **Click the Delete layer button 🗑 in the Layers palette**

   A warning box appears, as shown in Figure E-15. This dialog box allows you to choose whether you want to apply the layer mask to the layer before you discard it. If you choose Discard, you will eliminate the layer mask for the Rainbow layer.

5. **Click Discard**

   The Rainbow layer mask is removed from the document, as shown in Figure E-16.

> **QuickTip**
>
> You can temporarily disable a layer mask by pressing [Shift], then clicking the Layer mask thumbnail.

6. **Click Edit on the menu bar, then click Undo Discard Layer Mask**

   The Rainbow layer mask is restored to the document.

7. **Click File on the menu bar, then click Save**

FIGURE E-14: Layer mask disabled

Disabled layer mask

FIGURE E-15: Warning box

Click to apply mask to layer before removing

Click to remove mask without applying to layer

FIGURE E-16: Image with layer mask removed

Layer has original appearance

Layer mask removed

Photoshop 6.0

Photoshop 6.0

Adding an Adjustment Layer

You can experiment with changing a document's appearance without making permanent modifications by creating an adjustment layer. An **adjustment layer** is an additional layer for which you can specify 11 color adjustments. These color adjustments are described in detail in Table E-1. The type of adjustment you choose determines the effects of the adjustment layer which acts as a screen, allowing underlying layers to appear. Adding one or more adjustment layers to a document lets you see the effects of adjusting colors on layers without making a permanent commitment. You could, for example, add two adjustment layers—both for Brightness/Contrast—to a layer, then hide and show each one to view the effects of each adjustment layer and decide which you think is more effective. A unique icon ▣ identifies the adjustment layer in the Layers palette. ✎ Jan wants to create an adjustment layer above the Rainbow Fruit & Nuts layer to view it with more brightness and contrast.

Steps

1. Click the **Rainbow Fruit & Nuts layer** in the Layers palette

QuickTip

You can also create a new adjustment layer by clicking the Create new fill or adjustment layer button ▣ in the Layers palette, then selecting a color adjustment.

2. Click **Layer** on the menu bar, point to **New Adjustment Layer**, then click **Brightness/Contrast**
   The New Layer dialog box opens, as shown in Figure E-17. The New Adjustment Layer command on the Layer menu can be used to make the following adjustments: Levels, Curves, Color Balance, Brightness/Contrast, Hue/Saturation, Selective Color, Channel Mixer, Gradient Map, Invert, Threshold, and Posterize. The default name of the adjustment layer is taken from the type of color adjustment you selected.

QuickTip

Create multiple adjustment layers if you need to make several types of modifications.

3. Click **OK**
   The Brightness/Contrast dialog box opens, and a new layer, called Brightness/Contrast 1, appears above the Rainbow Fruit & Nuts layer in the Layers palette.

QuickTip

You can change the adjustment layer settings by double-clicking ▣ on the adjustment layer.

4. Type **-15** in the Brightness text box, then type **+30** in the Contrast text box
   Compare your settings to Figure E-18.

5. Click **OK**
   Notice that the images in the document appear brighter.

6. Make sure that the **Brightness/Contrast 1 layer** is still the active layer, click the **Set the blending mode list arrow** in the Layers palette, then click **Soft Light**
   Compare your image to Figure E-19.

7. Click **File** on the menu bar, then click **Save**

Merging adjustment layers

You can merge adjustment layers with any *visible* layers in the image, including linked layers or layers in a clipping group. You cannot, however, merge one adjustment layer with another adjustment layer. Merging the adjustment layers reduces file size and ensures that your adjustments will be permanent.

FIGURE E-17: New Layer dialog box

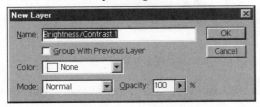

FIGURE E-18: Brightness/Contrast dialog box

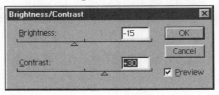

FIGURE E-19: Results of adjustment layer

Indicates adjustment layer

TABLE E-1: Common color adjustments

color adjustment	description
Levels	Sets highlights and shadows in a document by increasing the tonal range of pixels, while preserving the color balance
Curves	Makes adjustments to a document's entire tonal range using three variables: highlights, shadows, and midtones
Color Balance	Changes the overall mixture of color
Brightness/Contrast	Makes simple adjustments to a document's tonal range
Hue/Saturation	Changes position on the color wheel (hue) or purity of a color (saturation)
Selective Color	Increases or decreases the number of process colors in each of the additive and subtractive primary color components
Channel Mixer	Modifies a color channel using a mix of current color channels
Gradient Map	Maps the equivalent grayscale range of an image to colors of a specific gradient fill
Invert	Converts an image's brightness values to its inverse value on the 256-step color-values scale
Threshold	Converts images to high-contrast, black-and-white images
Posterize	Specifies the number of tonal levels for each channel

Photoshop 6.0

Creating a Clipping Group

A **clipping group** is a group of two or more contiguous layers (layers that are next to each other in the Layers palette). Clipping groups are useful when you want one layer to act as the mask for other layers. The bottom layer in a clipping group is called the **base layer** and it serves as the group's mask. The properties of the base layer determine the opacity and visible imagery of a clipping group. You can, however, adjust the opacity of the individual layers in a clipping group. The name of the base layer is underlined, and each thumbnail for the additional grouped layers appears indented. Jan wants to combine two layers into a clipping group so that the layer above it will use the characteristics of the base layer.

Steps

1. Click the **Background layer** in the Layers palette
This layer will serve as the base layer of the clipping group.

2. Press and hold **Alt (Win)** or **Option (Mac)**, then move the pointer to the **line between the Background layer and the Rainbow layer**
The pointer changes to ◄🖐, as shown in Figure E-20.

QuickTip

You can remove the effects of a clipping group by selecting the base layer, clicking Layer on the menu bar, then clicking Ungroup.

3. When the pointer changes to ◄🖐, click the **line between the two layers**
A downward pointing black arrow ⬇ appears to the left of the Layer thumbnail on each layer (above the base layer) in the clipping group. Compare your final project with Figure E-21. Notice that the Background layer is underlined, and that the Rainbow Layer thumbnail is indented. When a clipping group is created, portions of a layer in the group may disappear because the clipping group takes on the opacity and mode attributes of the base layer.

QuickTip

You can use a type layer as the base of a clipping group so that a pattern appears through the text.

4. Type your name in the lower-right corner of the image

5. Click the **Move Tool** 🖐, then **save** your work

6. Click **File** on the menu bar, click **Save As**, then using the name given, click the **As a Copy check box**, then click **Save**
A copy of the document with all the layers intact is created and closed.

7. Click **Layer** on the menu bar, then click **Flatten Image**
The document is now flattened—having only one layer—and takes up less disk space.

Trouble?

If you receive a warning box when you print the document, click Proceed to continue.

8. **Save** the document, then **print** one copy of it

9. **Exit (Win)** or **Quit (Mac)** Photoshop

FIGURE E-20: Creating a clipping group

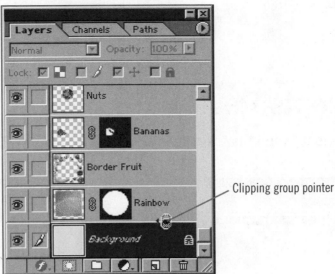

Clipping group pointer

FIGURE E-21: The finished project

Indicates layer is part
of a clipping group

Clipping group
base layer

Photoshop 6.0

Practice

▶ Concepts Review

Label each element in the Photoshop window shown in Figure E-22.

FIGURE E-22

Match each button, tool, or pointer with the statement that describes its function.

7. ▢
8. ◂▢
9. ▣
10. ▤
11. ▣
12. ◭

a. Indicates an adjustment layer
b. Creates clipping group
c. Mask icon
d. This Layer slider
e. Link icon
f. Adds a layer mask

Select the best answer from the list of choices.

13. You can determine each of the following attributes from the Layers palette, *except* the
    a. Link status.
    b. Opacity.
    c. Brightness.
    d. Clipping group.

14. Which symbol indicates that you can edit a layer mask?
    a.
    b.
    c.
    d.

15. Which tool is used to paint a layer mask?
    a.
    b.
    c.
    d.

16. Which pointer appears when creating a clipping group?
    a.
    b.
    c.
    d.

17. Which button is used to create an adjustment layer?
    a.
    b.
    c.
    d.

18. A combined series of layers is called a(n)
    a. Adjustment layer.
    b. Clipping group.
    c. Joined layer.
    d. Arrangement.

19. Which icon appears when you can edit a layer?
    a.
    b.
    c.
    d.

Photoshop 6.0

20. **The base layer in a clipping group is shown**
    a. In bold.
    b. In italics.
    c. In upper-case letters.
    d. Underlined.

21. **When you edit a layer mask, the foreground and background colors default to**
    a. Grayscale values.
    b. The currently selected foreground and background colors.
    c. The foreground and background colors active when Photoshop opened.
    d. Red and blue.

If you receive a warning box when you print any of the end of unit exercises, click Proceed to continue.

► Skills Review

1. **Create a layer mask.**
    a. Start Photoshop.
    b. Open PS E-2, then save it as *Stripes*.
    c. Make sure the rulers appear in pixels.
    d. Zoom in to 150%.
    e. Click the Zebra layer.
    f. Select the Elliptical Marquee Tool on the toolbox.
    g. Change the Feather setting on the tool options bar to 5 pixels.
    h. Create a marquee selection from 35 H/35 V to 235 H/360 V.
    i. Click the Add a mask button in the Layers palette.
    j. Save your work.

2. **Paint a layer mask.**
    a. Select the Paintbrush Tool on the toolbox.
    b. Click the Painting Brush list arrow on the tool options bar, then click the second brush tip from the left in the second row.
    c. Verify that the Painting mode is set to Normal, and that the Opacity setting is 100% on the tool options bar.
    d. Click the Layer mask thumbnail on the Zebra layer.
    e. Verify that the default foreground and background colors have been set.
    f. Paint the area from 20 H/70 V to 55 H/290 V.
    g. Save your work.

3. **Link and unlink layers.**
    a. Make the Fern layer active.
    b. Click the link icon on the Background layer to unlink the layer.
    c. Click the link icon on the type layer.
    d. Click the empty gray square to the left of the Layer thumbnail on the Background layer again to link the layer.
    e. Save your work.

4. Blend pixels between layers.
   a. Double-click the Fern layer.
   b. Drag the left This Layer slider until the display reads 91.
   c. Click OK.
   d. Save your work.

5. Remove layer mask.
   a. Click the Layer mask thumbnail on the Zebra layer.
   b. Disable the layer mask on the Zebra layer.
   c. Use the Layer menu to enable the layer mask.
   d. Save your work.

6. Add an adjustment layer.
   a. Make the Fern layer active.
   b. Create a Color Balance adjustment layer called **Modifications**.
   c. Make sure the Midtones option button is selected, then drag the Cyan, Magenta, and Yellow sliders to +36, +12, and -19, respectively.
   d. Create a Brightness/Contrast adjustment layer above the Modifications layer called **Brightness/Contrast**.
   e. Change the Brightness to -25 and the Contrast to +20.
   f. Click the eye button on the Modifications layer. Observe the difference in the document.
   g. Click the Show/Hide Layer button on the Modifications layer. Click the eye button on the Brightness/Contrast layer. Observe the difference in the document.
   h. Make sure both adjustment layers are visible.
   i. Save your work.

7. Create a clipping group.
   a. Make the Background layer active.
   b. Press and hold Alt (Win) or Option (Mac), then create a clipping group (with the Background layer as the base layer) that includes the type layer and the Zebra layer.
   c. Type your name in the lower-left corner of the document.
   d. Save and print your work.
   e. Exit (Win) or Quit (Mac) Photoshop.

Photoshop 6.0

▶ Independent Challenges

1. A local modern art gallery hires you to promote its upcoming exhibit on the influences of technology in society. The gallery gives you an image to feature in the promotion, but the rest is up to you.

    a. Open PS E-3 from the drive and folder where your Project Files are stored, then save it as *Gallery Exhibit*.
    b. Apply a mask to the Sky layer.
    c. Add a type layer. Develop your own phrasing that will inspire people to come to the exhibit.
    d. Modify the blending mode on the Ball layer.
    e. Create at least one adjustment layer that modifies the contrast of the image.
    f. Type your name in the lower-left corner of the document.
    g. Save and print the document.

2. You are asked to teach an introductory course on Photoshop. Based on your knowledge of the program, develop an advertisement describing or illustrating the course. This advertisement will be reproduced in your institution's brochure.

    a. Create a Photoshop document with the dimensions 290 pixels × 360 pixels, then save it as *Photoshop Course*.
    b. Use any available images from the Project Files, those that come with Photoshop, or are on your computer.
    c. Create any necessary selections to drag the images from other files into the Photoshop Course document.
    d. Change the blending mode on at least one layer.
    e. Add at least one type layer. Develop your own phrasing that describes the course.
    f. Create a mask on at least one layer.
    g. Create at least one adjustment layer that modifies the image's appearance.
    h. Type your name in the lower-left corner of the document.
    i. Save and print the document.

3. You decide to enter a local competition for graphic artists. This competition is open to all artwork created using a computer graphic imaging program.

a. Find several images—photographs or advertisements—that you think would be interesting in a Photoshop document, then scan and save them.

b. Create a Photoshop document with the dimensions 480 pixels × 480 pixels, then save it as *Competition*.

c. Create any necessary selections to drag portions of the scanned images into the Competition document.

d. Change the blending mode on at least one layer.

e. Create a mask on at least one layer.

f. Create at least one adjustment layer that modifies the image's appearance.

g. Type your name in the lower-left corner of the document.

h. Create at least one clipping group with at least two layers.

i. Save and print the image.

4. You have been asked to create an exciting new effect using a blending mode. Using resources on the Web, you can learn new Photoshop techniques.
To complete this independent challenge:

a. Go to the Northern Light search engine at *http://www.northernlight.com* and enter: Photoshop blending modes. You can also use Yahoo!, Excite, Infoseek, or another search engine of your choice.

b. Locate and visit at least one tutorial or article on blending modes, then print out the page(s).

c. Go to *http://www.photoshop-cafe.com/*.

d. Click the link for Tutorials, click the link for Splattered Drop Shadow, then print the instructions. (*Hint*: follow the directions to create this effect.)

e. Create a Photoshop document called *Splattered* with the dimensions 360 pixels × 280 pixels.

f. Use the instructions to create any necessary layers, including a type layer with your name.

g. Apply any additional techniques you feel are necessary to create a professional image.

h. Save and print this document.

Photoshop 6.0

Photoshop 6.0 *Practice*

▶ Visual Workshop

Open PS E-4 from the drive and folder where your Project Files are stored, and save it as *Everything Electrical*. Use the skills you learned in this unit to modify the document so it looks like Figure E-23. The adjustment layer should control Color Balance using the following settings: Cyan = -30, Magenta = -10, and Yellow = +35. Modify the Name layer so it contains your name. Print the document.

FIGURE E-23

Photoshop 6.0

Unit F

Creating
Special Effects with Filters

Objectives

▶ **Understand filters**
▶ **Apply a Blur filter**
▶ **Use an Artistic filter**
▶ **Stylize an image**
▶ **Twirl a layer**
▶ **Understand lighting effects**
▶ **Apply lighting effects**
▶ **Apply a texture**

A filter alters the look of an image by customizing it. Once you place layers in an image, you are ready to apply special effects to the imagery. You use **filters** to apply special effects, such as distortions, changes in lighting, and blurring. You know how a Blur filter can soften the appearance of type; now you will learn how other effects can be created using Photoshop filters. ✎━━ Wendy Fleming is a Department Manager at Zenith Design. Her new client, the All-Romance Network, is a recent addition to the cable television line-up. The All-Romance Network plans to launch a daytime drama next year. Wendy discussed the advertising campaign design with the executive producer. She is ready to finalize the opening image so it can be published in "Soap Digest."

Understanding Filters

There are 14 categories of Photoshop filters on the Filter menu. Each category contains several filters. When you click Distort, for example, under the Filter menu, you can choose one of 12 ways to distort a layer, including Diffuse Glow, Ocean Ripple, or Twirl. Filters, which are applied to layers, add unique and dramatic effects to your image. Some filters give the illusion of light, depth or texture to a layer. Some filters show you how the layer will be affected by the filter in a preview window *before* you apply the filter. Other filter effects can only be seen in the document *after* you apply the filter. Some filters require a lot of memory, so using them may slow down your computer's performance. Before she changes the image, Wendy reviews the many filters available in Photoshop.

Details

Artistic and Blur filters

Use an Artistic filter to replicate natural or traditional effects. You can apply effects such as Colored Pencil, Dry Brush, Film Grain, Plastic Wrap, Sponge, or Fresco. The Plastic Wrap filter was applied to the Lobster layer in Figure F-1. Use a Blur filter, such as Gaussian Blur, Motion Blur, or Radial Blur, to soften a selection or image. A Motion Blur was applied to the Fortune Cookie layer in Figure F-1.

Brush Strokes and Distort filters

Like the Artistic filters, the Brush Strokes filter mimics fine arts brushwork. Examples of Brush Strokes filters include Accented Edges, Crosshatch, and Spatter. A Distort filter creates three-dimensional or other reshaping effects. Examples of Distort filters include Glass, Pinch, Shear, and Twirl. In Figure F-1, the Twirl filter was applied to the Clouds layer.

Noise and Pixelate filters

Noise filters add or remove pixels with randomly distributed color levels to give an aged look to retouched photographs. Filters in this category include Add Noise, Despeckle, and Dust and Scratches. Pixelate filters, such as Crystallize, Mosaic, and Pointillize, sharply define a selection. The Pointillize filter is shown in Figure F-2.

Render and Sharpen filters

Render filters allow you to transform three-dimensional shapes and simulated light reflections in an image. Filters in this category include 3-D Transform, Clouds, and Lighting Effects. Sharpen filters bring blurry objects into focus by increasing the contrast in adjacent pixels. Examples include Sharpen, Sharpen More, and Unsharp Mask filters. The Sharpen More filter is shown in Figure F-3.

Sketch and Stylize filters

A Sketch filter applies a texture, or simulates a hand-drawn effect. Examples of Sketch filters include Chrome, Graphic Pen, and Stamp. Stylize filters produce a painted or impressionistic effect. Examples of Stylize filters include Diffuse, Solarize, and Wind.

Texture and Video filters

Texture filters give the appearance of depth or substance. These filters include Craquelure, Mosaic Tiles, and Stained Glass. Video filters restrict colors to those that are acceptable for television reproduction and smooth video images. The Craquelure filter was applied to the Rose layer in Figure F-1.

Digimarc and Other filters

Digimarc filters embed a digital watermark that stores copyright information into an image. You can apply the Other filters category to create your own filters, modify masks, or make quick color adjustments to layers, or portions of existing layers.

FIGURE F-1: Filters applied to layers

Effect of Craquelure filter

Effect of Motion Blur filter

Effect of Twirl filter

Effect of Plastic Wrap filter

FIGURE F-2: Pointillize filter

Effect of Pointillize Filter

FIGURE F-3: Sharpen More filter

Effect of Sharpen More Filter

Applying a Blur Filter

A Blur filter can be used to suggest motion in a selection or on a layer. A Blur filter can also soften an image. Each Blur filter produces a different effect. The **Motion Blur** filter adjusts the angle of the blur, as well as the distance the blur appears to travel. The **Radial Blur** filter adjusts the amount of blur and the blur method (Spin or Zoom). The **Smart Blur** filter adjusts the quality, radius, and threshold of the blur. ✎ Wendy wants to soften the Fortune Cookie image, then give it a sense of motion. She will apply the Motion Blur filter to the Fortune Cookie layer.

Steps

1. Start Photoshop, open **PS F-1** from the drive and folder where your Project Files are stored, then save the file as **Soap Opera**

2. Click the **Default Foreground and Background Colors button** ▣ on the toolbox, if necessary, click **View** on the menu bar, then click **Show Rulers**, if necessary
   It's a good idea to check Photoshop settings and display the rulers before you begin your work. The foreground and background colors now display the default settings.

3. Click the **Fortune Cookie layer** in the Layers palette
   The Fortune Cookie layer is active. You can now apply a filter to it.

4. Click **Filter** on the menu bar, point to **Blur**, then click **Motion Blur**
   The Motion Blur dialog box opens. Each filter dialog box has Zoom in ⊞ and Zoom out ⊟ buttons directly below the preview window that you can click to see more or less of the active layer. Zooming in gives you a closer look at the changes you make. You can also use ✋ to move the image within the preview window.

QuickTip
The last filter applied to a layer appears at the top of the Filter menu.

5. Use ⊟ and ⊞, and ✋ to position the fortune cookie, as shown in Figure F-4
   Changes that you make in filter dialog boxes automatically appear in the preview window.

6. Type **3** in the **Angle** text box, then type **5** in the **Distance** text box
   You can also adjust the settings in the Motion Blur dialog box by dragging the Angle radius slider and Distance slider. The fortune cookie appears with a slight blur. Compare your dialog box to Figure F-5.

7. Click **OK**
   The Motion Blur filter is applied to the Fortune Cookie layer, as shown in Figure F-6.

8. Click **File** on the menu bar, then click **Save**

Applying a filter to a selection

You can specify a particular area of a layer to which you want to apply a filter. To do so, you can use a selection tool, such as the Rectangular Marquee Tool ▫ or the Elliptical Marquee Tool ◯, to define an area, then apply the desired filter. The filter will be applied only to the selected area, not the entire layer. If you wish to apply a filter to a layer that contains a mask, be sure to select the layer name, not the Layer mask thumbnail.

FIGURE F-4: Positioned image in Motion Blur dialog box

Click button to zoom out

Click button to zoom in

Angle radius slider— alternate method to establish blur angle

Distance slider— determines the length of blur

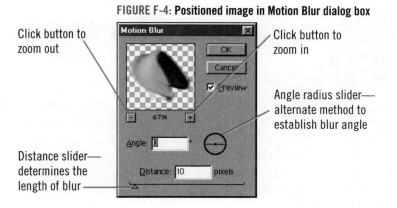

FIGURE F-5: Modified Motion Blur settings

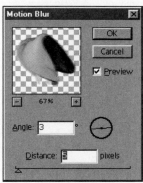

FIGURE F-6: Motion Blur filter applied to layer

Effect of Motion Blur filter

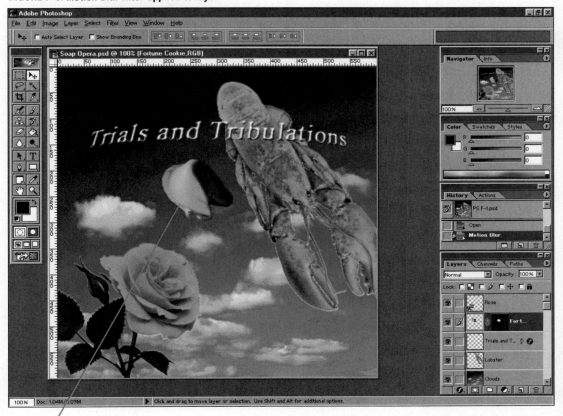

Photoshop 6.0

Using an Artistic Filter

You can dramatically alter an image using Artistic filters. **Artistic filters** are often used for special effects in television commercials. The Plastic Wrap filter, for example, makes the contents of a layer look as though they are covered in plastic, and tends to accentuate surface details. Other Artistic filters include Film Grain, which applies even color variations throughout an object, and Watercolor, which simplifies the appearance of an object making it look like it was painted with watercolors. ◢━━ Wendy wants to distort the edges of the Lobster layer. She begins by hiding distracting layers.

1. Click the **Lobster layer** in the Layers palette

QuickTip

Hide any distracting layers while modifying a document.

2. Click the **eye button** 👁 on the **Trials and Tribulations layer** in the Layers palette
The Trials and Tribulations layer no longer appears, as shown in Figure F-7.

3. Click **Filter** on the menu bar, point to **Artistic**, then click **Plastic Wrap**
The Plastic Wrap dialog box opens.

QuickTip

Move the Plastic Wrap dialog box if it obscures your view.

4. Type **9** in the **Highlight Strength** text box, type **11** in the **Detail** text box, then type **9** in the **Smoothness** text box
Your settings should look like those in Figure F-8. The Plastic Wrap filter is extremely memory-intensive. Your computer's performance may diminish after you apply this filter.

5. Click **OK**
The Lobster layer displays the effects of the Plastic Wrap filter, as shown in Figure F-9.

Trouble?

Your foreground and background colors may differ.

6. Click the **Show/Hide layer button** ▢ on the **Trials and Tribulations layer** in the Layers palette
The type layer appears.

7. Click **File** on the menu bar, then click **Save**

Controlling brightness and contrast

You can maximize the effects of a filter by controlling the brightness and contrast of a layer. Before applying a filter to the active layer, click Image on the menu bar, point to Adjust, then click Brightness/Contrast. Drag the Brightness and Contrast sliders until you achieve the desired effect, then apply the filter.

FIGURE F-7: Type layer hidden

Hidden layer   Active layer

FIGURE F-8: Plastic Wrap dialog box

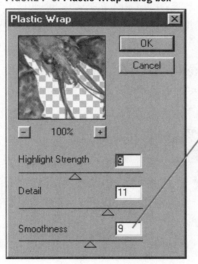

A higher value produces a smoother appearance

FIGURE F-9: Plastic Wrap filter applied to layer

Effect of Plastic Wrap filter

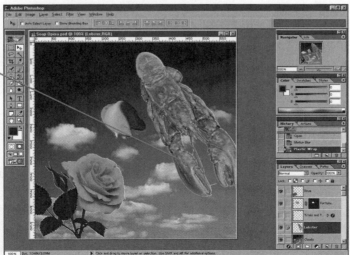

Photoshop 6.0

Stylizing an Image

Stylize filters produce a painted or impressionistic effect by displacing pixels and heightening the contrast within an image. Some filters, such as the **Wind filter**, convey the feeling of direction and motion. The **Diffuse filter** makes layer contents look less focused, according to whether you want the objects lighter or darker. The **Darken Only** option replaces light pixels with darker pixels, while the **Lighten Only** option replaces dark pixels with light pixels. Wendy will use the Diffuse filter to give the edges of the rose a darker appearance, and the Wind filter to give the rose the feeling of direction.

Steps

1. Click the **Rose layer** in the Layers palette
   The Rose layer is active.

2. Click **Filter** on the menu bar, point to **Stylize**, then click **Diffuse**
   The Diffuse dialog box opens.

Trouble?

You may not see the rose in the preview window until you click the Zoom out button and use to adjust your view.

3. Verify that the **Preview check box** is selected, then use the **Zoom out button**, the **Zoom in button**, and to position the rose in the preview window, as shown in Figure F-10

4. Click the **Darken Only option button**, then click **OK**
   The Diffuse filter is applied to the Rose layer.

QuickTip

You can also create a visual association between different images by applying a similar set of filters to them.

5. Click **Filter** on the menu bar, point to **Stylize**, then click **Wind**
   The Wind dialog box opens.

6. Use and , and to position the rose in the center of the preview window

7. Click the **From the Left option button** in the Direction section of the Wind dialog box.
   Compare your settings to Figure F-11.

8. Click **OK**
   The Rose layer gives the illusion that wind is blowing from the left. Compare your image to Figure F-12.

9. Click **File** on the menu bar, then click **Save**

Using filters to enhance images

You can use filters to disguise imperfections in an image. Applying a filter can make an imperfection less noticeable by enhancing an area within an image that is less than attractive. By applying a filter to a muddy or blurred area of an image, you can turn an image defect into an asset.

FIGURE F-10: Diffuse dialog box

FIGURE F-11: Wind dialog box

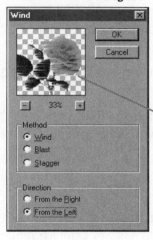

Changes appear on image as they are made

FIGURE F-12: Wind filter applied to layer

Effect of Wind filter

Twirling a Layer

The **Twirl filter** in the Distort category applies a circular effect to a layer. By adjusting the angle of the twirl, you can make images look as if they are moving or spinning. Any changes that you make in the Twirl dialog box will automatically appear in the preview window, but not in the image. ✐ Wendy wants to use the Twirl filter to suggest movement on the Clouds layer. She starts by hiding distracting layers in the image.

Steps

1. Click the **eye button** 👁 on the **Fortune Cookie layer** in the Layers palette
   The Fortune Cookie layer is no longer visible.

2. Click the 👁 on the **Rose layer** and **Lobster layer** in the Layers palette
   The Rose and Lobster layers are no longer visible.

3. Click the **Clouds layer** in the Layers palette
   The Clouds layer becomes the active layer. Compare your image to Figure F-13.

4. Click **Filter** on the menu bar, point to **Distort**, then click **Twirl**
   The Twirl dialog box opens. You can adjust the angle of the twirl by dragging the slider, or typing a value in the Angle text box.

5. Click the **Zoom out button** ⊟ to zoom out to 20%, then type **115** in the Angle text box
   The clouds appear to move in a circular motion. Compare your settings to Figure F-14.

6. Click **OK**
   The clouds now appear to twirl clockwise.

7. Click the **Show/Hide layer button** ⬜ on the **Fortune Cookie layer**, the **Rose layer**, and the **Lobster layer**
   All layers are now visible, as shown in Figure F-15.

8. Click **File** on the menu bar, then click **Save**

FIGURE F-13: **Three layers hidden**

Fortune Cookie layer

Layers hidden from view

FIGURE F-14: **Twirl dialog box**

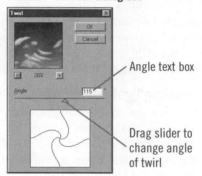

Angle text box

Drag slider to change angle of twirl

FIGURE F-15: **Twirl filter applied to layer**

Effect of Twirl filter

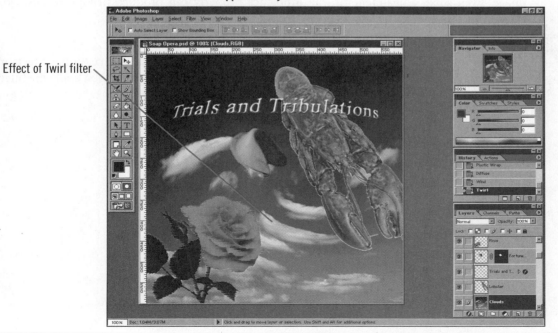

Understanding Lighting Effects

The type and source of lighting can alter and enhance the appearance of an image. You can use the **Lighting Effects filter** in the Render category to apply lighting effects to an image. The type and source of light can greatly affect a document's appearance. The Lighting Effects filter lets you determine one of three Light Types—Directional, Omni, or Spotlight—and adjust each type's intensity and focus. You can also adjust the properties of the surrounding light conditions. ✐ Before applying a lighting effect, Wendy reviews the options available in the Lighting Effects filter.

Details

Lighting Effects dialog box

The Lighting Effects dialog box contains several list arrows and sliders you can use to modify the lighting effect, as shown in Figure F-16. The preview window contains an ellipse that shows the direction and number of light sources. You can drag the handles on each ellipse to change the direction and distance of the light sources. The changes you make in the Lighting Effects dialog box automatically appear in the preview window.

Make light adjustments

You can adjust the brightness of the light by using the Intensity slider. Full intensity creates the brightest light; a Negative setting adds darkness. You can use the Focus slider to adjust the size of the beam of light filling the ellipse. The light source begins where the radius touches the edge of the ellipse. The three light types are shown in Figure F-17.

Adjust surrounding light conditions

You can adjust the surrounding light conditions using the Gloss, Material, Exposure, or Ambience properties, as shown in Figure F-18. The **Gloss** property controls the amount of surface reflectance on the lighted surfaces. The **Material** property controls the parts of an image that reflect the light source color; its effects range from plastic (glare) to metallic (glow). The **Exposure** property lightens or darkens the ellipse (the area displaying the light source). The **Ambience** property controls the balance between the light source and the overall light in an image. Even small adjustments in the Ambience property can produce striking results. The **Properties color swatch** changes the ambient light around the spotlight.

System requirements

Although the Lighting Effects filter is memory-intensive, it can produce exceptional effects in your image. Be aware that your computer's performance may diminish after you apply the filter.

FIGURE F-16: Lighting Effects dialog box

Preview window shows effects of settings

Light source

Ellipse shows light source and direction

Drag handles to change direction and distance of light source

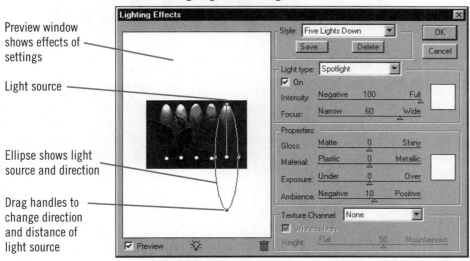

FIGURE F-17: Light types displayed in Lighting Effects dialog box

Available light types

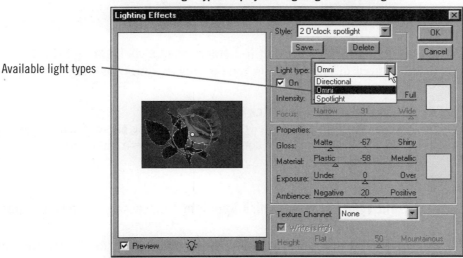

FIGURE F-18: Properties in the Lighting Effects dialog box

List of available lighting styles

Lighting Effects properties

Properties color swatch

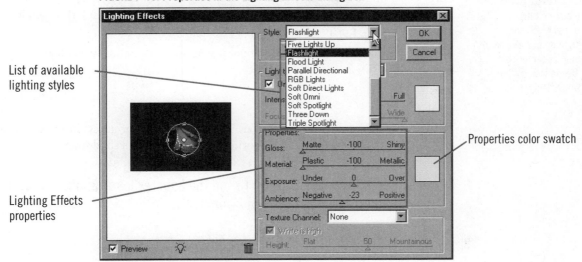

Photoshop 6.0

Applying Lighting Effects

You can change the overall mood and tone of an image by applying lighting effects to it. After selecting the desired light style and light type, you can manipulate the direction and distance of the light. You can change the origin and position of the lighting by dragging the handles on the ellipse in the Lighting Effects preview window. The apparent distance of the light is equivalent to the distance of the ellipse handles to the image. Wendy wants to change the style, distance, and direction of the lighting in the document.

1. Make sure the **Clouds layer** is active

2. Click the **eye button** 👁 on the **Lobster layer** and **Rose layer** in the Layers palette
   The Lobster layer and Rose layer are no longer visible. You want to hide layers while you adjust the lighting.

3. Click **Filter** on the menu bar, point to **Render**, then click **Lighting Effects**
   The Lighting Effects dialog box opens. You can choose from 17 lighting styles.

QuickTip

You can eliminate the ellipse to change the effects of the lighting filter by dragging the light bulb icon 💡 into the preview window.

4. Click the **Style list arrow**, then click **Crossing Down**
   The preview window displays the newly selected style. The ellipse for the Crossing Down style shows the direction of the light coming from the upper-right corner.

QuickTip

Lighting effects must include at least one light source.

5. Click the **Light Type list arrow**, click **Spotlight** if necessary, then verify that the **On check box** is selected
   The preview window shows the changed Spotlight light source. You can use the handles on the ellipse to change the shape and direction of the light source.

QuickTip

When there are multiple sources of light, you can delete a light source ellipse by dragging its center point over the Delete icon 🗑 in the Lighting Effects dialog box.

6. Enter the same slider settings in the Lighting Effects dialog box, shown in Figure F-19, and drag the **top elliptical handle** to the upper-left edge of the preview box, also shown in Figure F-19
   As you drag the ellipse handle, the preview window automatically displays the change in the lighting direction and distance.

7. Click **OK**
   The lighting in the document changes. The light appears brightest in the upper-left corner, and the lower-left and upper-right corners appear to be in a shadow.

8. Click the **Show/Hide layer button** ▣ on the **Lobster layer** and **Rose layer**
   All layers become visible, as shown in Figure F-20.

9. Click **File** on the menu bar, then click **Save**

FIGURE F-19: Changing settings in the Lighting Effects dialog box

Drag handle to edge of preview box

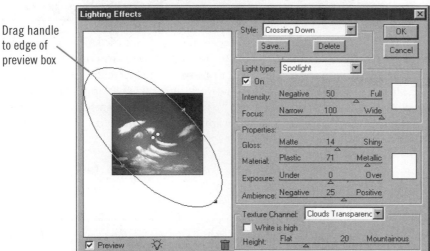

FIGURE F-20: Lighting Effects filter applied to layer

Light comes from upper-left side

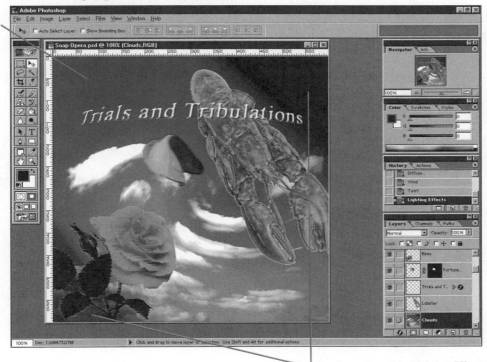

Shadows caused by Lighting Effects filter

Creating custom lighting effects

As you modify a style in the Lighting Effects dialog box, you can save the settings as a new style with a unique name. To create a custom style, choose your settings, then click the Save button beneath the Style list arrow. Enter a new name in the Save as dialog box, then click OK. The new style name will appear alphabetically in the Style list. You can delete an entry by selecting it from the Style list, then clicking the Delete button.

CLUES TO USE

Photoshop 6.0

Applying a Texture

Texture filters can be used to give an image an appearance of depth, or a grainy, organic look. You can apply them to an image layer or to the Background layer. If you want to apply a Texture filter to a type layer, you must rasterize it to convert it to an image layer. The Craquelure filter is in the Texture category and produces a network of cracks that appear to follow the contours of an object. The Craquelure filter can also be used to create an embossing effect. ✐ Wendy wants to further modify the Rose layer by applying a texture to it.

Steps

1. Click the **Rose layer** in the Layers palette
   This layer was already blurred using the Wind filter. Now you can apply a Texture filter to the layer.

2. Click **Filter** on the menu bar, point to **Texture**, then click **Craquelure**
   The Craquelure dialog box opens.

3. Click the **Zoom out button** ⊟ to zoom out to 50%
   The rose becomes visible in the preview box.

4. Type **16** in the **Crack Spacing** text box, type **3** in the **Crack Depth** text box, then type **7** in the **Crack Brightness** text box
   Compare your settings to Figure F-21.

5. Click **OK**
   The Craquelure filter is applied to the rose, as shown in the finished document in Figure F-22.

6. Type your name in the lower-right corner of the image, then click the **Move Tool** ⊕ on the toolbox

7. Click **File** on the menu bar, then click **Save**

Trouble?

If a warning box opens, click Proceed.

8. Print **one copy** of the document

9. **Exit (Win)** or **Quit (Mac)** Photoshop

FIGURE F-21: Craquelure dialog box

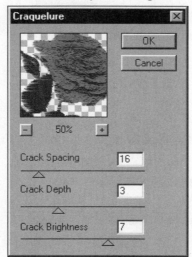

FIGURE F-22: The finished project

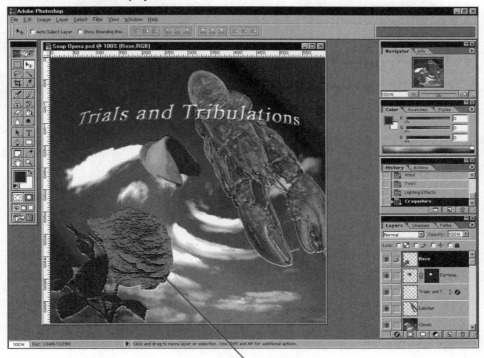

Effect of Craquelure filter

Undoing the application of a filter

The last filter applied to a layer becomes the first menu item at the top of the Filter menu. You can click it to apply the same filter to another layer using the identical settings chosen in the Filter dialog box. If you mistakenly apply a filter to the wrong layer, you can easily correct your error by clicking Edit on the menu bar, then clicking Undo (*Filter name*). Make sure the correct layer is active, click Filter on the menu bar, then click the top entry. The filter—and the most recent settings—will be applied to the active layer.

Practice

▶ Concepts Review

Label each filter effect in the Photoshop window shown in Figure F-23.

FIGURE F-23

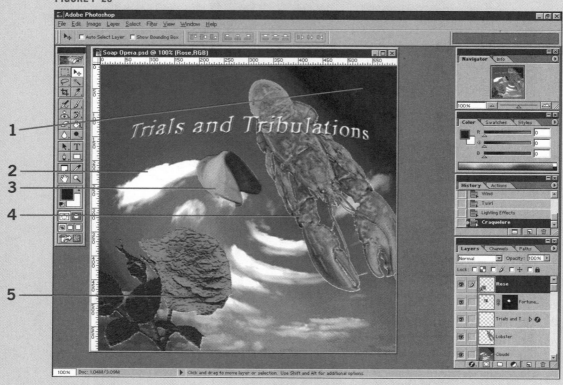

Match each button, tool, pointer, or phrase with the statement that describes its function.

6. Deletes or restores a light source ellipse
7. Hides a layer
8. Gives appearance of depth
9. Intensity slider
10. Creates circular effect
11. Removes ellipse

a. Adjusts light brightness
b. Twirl filter
c. 💡
d. 👁
e. Texture filter
f. 🗑

Select the best answer from the list of choices.

12. Which menu is used to apply a filter?
   a. File
   b. Edit
   c. Layer
   d. Filter

13. Which of the following is *not* a filter category?
   a. Sharpen
   b. Texture
   c. Glass
   d. Noise

14. You can change the direction of lighting effects using the
   a. Lighting menu.
   b. Handles on the ellipse.
   c. 💡.
   d. Direction dialog box.

15. Which filter category works best to soften an image?
   a. Render
   b. Digimarc
   c. Blur
   d. Noise

16. Which filter category works best to create three-dimensional effects?
   a. Noise
   b. Pixelate
   c. Distort
   d. Artistic

17. Which lighting property controls the amount of light that is reflected from the surface?
   a. Properties
   b. Ambience
   c. Gloss
   d. Sunshine

18. Which of the following is true about filters?
   a. A maximum of three filters can be applied to a layer.
   b. Only one filter can be applied to a layer.
   c. Any number of filters can be applied to a layer.
   d. A maximum of five filters can be applied to a layer.

19. Which filter is *not* a member of the Texture category?
   a. Stained Glass
   b. Film Grain
   c. Mosaic Tiles
   d. Craquelure

20. Which filter is *not* a member of the Noise category?
   a. Despeckle
   b. Pointillize
   c. Dust and Scratches
   d. Add Noise

▶ Skills Review

1. **Apply a Blur filter.**
   a. Start Photoshop.
   b. Open PS F-2, then save it as *Concert Program*.
   c. Make sure the rulers appear.
   d. Make the Horn layer active.
   e. Hide any unnecessary or distracting layers.
   f. Apply a Motion Blur filter (in the Blur category) with the following settings: Angle = 2 and Distance = 2.
   g. Use the zoom tools in the filter's dialog box to completely view the layer's object in the preview box.
   h. Show any hidden layers.
   i. Save your work.

2. **Use an Artistic filter.**
   a. Make the CD-piano layer active.
   b. Hide any unnecessary or distracting layers.
   c. Open the Film Grain filter (in the Artistic category).
   d. Use the zoom tools in the filter's dialog box to completely view the layer's object in the preview box.
   e. Apply the filter using the following settings: Grain = 8, Highlight Area = 3, and Intensity = 4.
   f. Show any hidden layers.
   g. Save your work.

3. **Stylize an image.**
   a. Make the Guitar layer active.
   b. Hide any unnecessary or distracting layers.
   c. Apply a Tiles filter (in the Stylize category).
   d. Use the following settings: Number of Tiles = 7, Maximum Offset = 10%, and fill empty areas with inverse image.
   e. Show any hidden layers.
   f. Save your work.

4. **Twirl a layer.**
   a. Make the Horn layer active.
   b. Hide any unnecessary or distracting layers.
   c. Apply a Twirl filter (in the Distort category).
   d. Use the zoom tools in the filter's dialog box to completely view the layer's object in the preview box.
   e. Use an angle of -95 degrees.
   f. Show any hidden layers.
   g. Save your work.

5. Apply lighting effects.
  a. Make the Clouds layer active.
  b. Hide any unnecessary or distracting layers.
  c. Apply a Lighting Effects filter (in the Render category).
  d. Use the following settings: Style = Soft Spotlight and Light Type = Omni.
  e. Drag the ellipse so that the central light source is in the upper-right corner of the image, as seen in Figure F-24.
  f. Show any hidden layers.
  g. Save your work.

FIGURE F-24

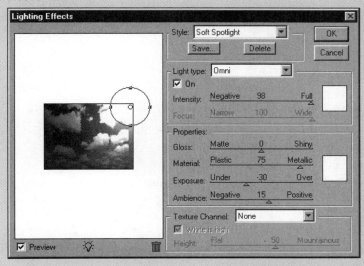

6. Apply a texture.
  a. Make the Notes layer active.
  b. Hide any unnecessary or distracting layers.
  c. Apply a Texturizer filter (in the Texture category).
  d. Use the zoom tools in the filter's dialog box to get a better view of the layer in the preview box.
  e. Use the following settings: Texture = Sandstone, Scaling = 50%, Relief = 10, and Light Direction = Top Right.
  f. Modify the Name layer by replacing Wendy's name with yours.
  g. Show any hidden layers.
  h. Save your work.
  i. Print one copy of the document.
  j. Exit (Win) or Quit (Mac) Photoshop.

Photoshop 6.0

► Independent Challenges

1. Your best friend is opening an antique shop and hires you to design a display ad that can be used in local print media. Because he'd like to attract high-end clientele, he wants the ad to look elegant and distinguished.

   a. Open PS F-3, then save it as *Antique Shop.*
   b. Locate and open at least one other Photoshop document on your computer.
   c. Create a selection in a second Photoshop document of your choice, then drag it to the Antique Shop file.
   d. Give the new layer (that contains the selection you dragged) a descriptive name.
   e. Apply a Blur or Distort filter to the Photos layer.
   f. Apply a filter to the new layer you created.
   g. If necessary, adjust the opacity of the layers.
   h. Add additional type layers or type styles, as necessary.
   i. Apply a Lighting Effects filter to at least one layer.
   j. Modify the Background layer using colors, if necessary.
   k. Modify the Name layer to include your name. (*Hint*: Change the location of the type layers, if necessary.)
   l. Save your work and print one copy of the document.

2. A travel agency is offering a vacation special to all its sales agents. The owner announced that whoever sells 200 airline tickets in one week will receive a free trip to an enchanting, warm, tropical island. Your co-workers unanimously decide that you should create the promotional poster for the sales office.

   a. Create a Photoshop document with the dimensions 290 pixels × 220 pixels, then save it as *Travel Poster*.
   b. Open Vacation.jpg from the drive and folder where your Project Files are stored.
   c. Create a selection within the Vacation document, then drag the selection to the Travel Poster document.
   d. Create a name for the new layer.
   e. Create any type layers and type styles you feel add to the image.
   f. Adjust the opacity of the layer, if necessary.
   g. Apply at least one filter to the image.
   h. Type your name in the lower-right corner of the document.
   i. Save your work and print one copy of the document.
   j. Save a flattened copy of the document using the default naming scheme.

3. The public relations department for your school's women's basketball team is sponsoring a design contest to increase attendance at games. The winning entry will appear on the cover of next season's program. You plan to enter—and win—this contest.

a. Locate and scan at least two images of your school or community that you feel would increase attendance at games. Save the scanned images in the drive and folder where your Project Files are stored.

b. Create a Photoshop document with the dimensions 290 pixels × 220 pixels, then save it as *Contest Image*.

c. Create any type layers you feel are appropriate. Apply any necessary formatting to the type layers.

d. Create a selection within the scanned image, then drag the selection to the Contest Image document.

e. Create a name for the new layer.

f. Apply at least one filter to each of the image layers in the Contest Image document.

g. Make opacity adjustments to any of the layers, as necessary.

h. Type your name in the lower-left corner of the document.

i. Save your work and print one copy of the document.

4. The Inside Photoshop Web site offers information about filter techniques. You can use this ever-changing resource to polish your skills.

a. Go to the Dogpile search engine at *http://www.dogpile.com* and enter: Photoshop filter techniques. You can also use Yahoo!, Excite, Infoseek, or another search engine of your choice.

b. Locate and visit at least one tutorial or article on filter techniques, then print out the page(s). For example, the Pixel Foundry site contains a tip on using a Gaussian Blur filter to remove a moiré pattern from images.

c. Open your favorite word processor, then save a new document as *Filter Technique* in the drive and folder where your Project Files are stored.

d. Using the information obtained from the Web pages, write a maximum of one page that summarizes your research. Be sure to reference your information source(s).

e. Add your name at the bottom of the document.

f. Save and print the document.

▶ # Visual Workshop

Open PS F-4 from the drive and folder where your Project Files are stored, then save the file as *Natural Beauty*. Use the skills you learned in this unit to modify the file so it looks like Figure F-25. Apply the Glass (Distort) filter to the Starfish layer mask using the following settings: Distortion = 10, Smoothness = 5, using a Canvas texture. Apply the Radial Blur (Blur) filter to the Water Drops layer using the following settings: Amount = 10, and the Spin Blur Method. Modify the Name layer by inserting your own name, save your work, then print the document.

FIGURE F-25

Unit **G**

Enhancing

a Document

Objectives

- ► **Understand channels**
- ► **Create an alpha channel**
- ► **Extract an object**
- ► **Fix a blemish**
- ► **Erase areas in an image**
- ► **Make specific selections**
- ► **Understand snapshots**
- ► **Create a multiple-image layout**

Your Photoshop skills now include adding type to an image, using masks to conceal areas, and using layers and filters to add dimension to a document. Additional Photoshop skills will help you enhance a document by fixing imperfections, making specific selections and creating multiple-image layouts. Zenith Design Intern Steve Gonzales was assigned the task of designing the cover for the California Fruit and Vegetable Growers Association catalog. Steve started work on a still-life image, to which he will apply several enhancing techniques.

Understanding Channels

Photoshop **channels** are used to store information about the color elements contained in each channel. For example, a **CMYK image** has at least four channels (one each for cyan, magenta, yellow, and black), whereas an **RGB image** has three channels (one each for red, green, and blue). Every Photoshop image has at least one channel, and can have a maximum of 24 color channels. The type of image determines the default number of color channels. The color channels contained in a document are known as **default channels.** You can add specific color information to a default channel by adding an **alpha channel.** Before he adds an alpha channel to his image, Steve reviews basic channel information.

Details

Automatic color information

Photoshop automatically creates channel information in a new document. The default number of channels is determined by which color mode you select in the New dialog box that opens when you create a new file, as shown in Figure G-1.

Alpha channels

You can also add an alpha channel to the default color channels. An alpha channel customizes an image by manipulating the appearance of specific areas. It creates a mask on a defined area on the layer. You can save alpha channels in the following formats (that support the document's color mode): Adobe Photoshop, PDF, PICT, TIFF, and Raw. Using other formats may cause the loss of some channel information.

QuickTip

To display the document size, click the List arrow ▶ on the status bar (Win) or document window (Mac), then click Document Sizes.

Channels and file size

Adding alpha channels increases the size of the file based on the mode that you select for the document. The file size appears as two values on the status bar (Win) or document window (Mac). The first number indicates the size of the file as a flattened file; the second number lists the file size if saved with all the layers and channels.

The Channels palette

The Channels palette lists all the default channels. To access this palette, click the Channels tab in the Layers palette, as shown in Figure G-2. The Channels palette manages the document's color channels. The top channel is a **composite channel**—a combination of all the default channels. You can hide channels in the same manner as you hide layers: Click the eye button 👁 in the column to the left of the Channel thumbnail.

FIGURE G-1: New dialog box

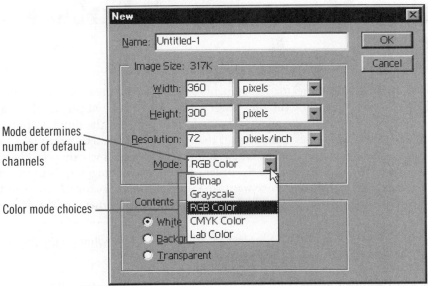

Mode determines number of default channels

Color mode choices

FIGURE G-2: Channels palette

Channels tab

Composite channel

Eye button

Default channels

CLUES TO USE

Displaying document information

The size of the open document normally appears on the status bar (Win) or the document window (Mac). However, you can choose to display other document information here, including Document Profile, Scratch Sizes, Efficiency, Timing, or Current Tool. The Document Profile setting shows information about the current color mode used by the document. The Scratch Sizes setting displays information about memory allocated to process a document. The Efficiency setting measures how quickly your computer processes commands, while the Timing setting displays the amount of time used to complete the last task. The Current Tool setting displays the name of the active tool on the toolbox.

Photoshop 6.0

Creating an Alpha Channel

You can create an alpha channel for a document to mask specific areas of a layer. The size of each alpha channel is determined by the file's color mode. As mentioned previously, channel information is listed in the Channels palette. Channels have many of the same properties as layers. For example, each channel has a thumbnail that mirrors the changes you make to the document's layers. A channel also contains an eye button that controls whether the channel appears in the document. You can also change the order of channels by dragging them to new locations in the Channels palette. ✎ Steve wants to enhance the image for the cover of the catalog. He will create an alpha channel that adds a frame around the perimeter of the document.

Steps

1. Start Photoshop, open **PS G-1** from the drive and folder where your Project Files are stored, then save the file as **Scrumptious**

2. Click the **Default Foreground and Background Colors button** ◨ on the toolbox, if necessary, click **View** on the menu bar, then click **Show Rulers**, if necessary
   The foreground and background colors now display the default settings.

3. Click the **Channels tab** ⟨Channels⟩ next to the Layers tab ⟨Layers⟩ in the Layers palette
   The Channels palette is active. Notice that there are four channels: RGB (composite), red, green, and blue, as shown in Figure G-3. You can create a new channel by using a selection tool.

4. Click the **Elliptical Marquee Tool** ◯ on the toolbox, then drag ╋ from **10 H/10 V to 685 H/580 V**
   A selection marquee in the shape of an ellipse appears on the image, as shown in Figure G-4. It will be used to define the channel mask.

5. Click the **Save selection as channel button** ▣ in the Channels palette
   A new channel, Alpha 1, appears at the bottom of the Channels palette. The channel mask takes on the shape of the elliptical selection marquee.

6. Click the **Show/Hide channel button** ▢ in the **Alpha 1 channel** in the Channels palette
   The area outside the selection (mask) appears as a gold transparent overlay because the channel appears in a red transparent color. The combination of red over yellow produces the gold color.

7. Click **Select** on the menu bar, then click **Deselect**
   The selection marquee disappears, as shown in Figure G-5.

8. Click **File** on the menu bar, then click **Save**

FIGURE G-3: Channels palette

Click to display the Channels palette

Composite channel

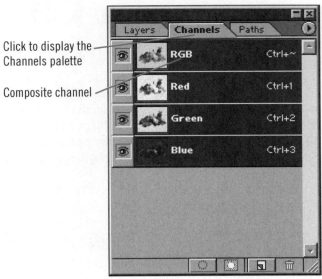

FIGURE G-4: Selection created

Elliptical Marquee Tool

Elliptical marquee

FIGURE G-5: Alpha channel created

Effect of Alpha 1 channel

Photoshop 6.0

Extracting an Object

Photoshop 6.0

The **Extract feature** can be used to isolate a foreground object from its background. This command lets you define the precise area that will be extracted. When you extract the selection, the remaining image is still visible. You can extract objects using a special tool to trace the outline you want to manipulate. If you make a mistake while tracing the outline, you can use Undo in the Edit menu to start over. Steve wants to extract the lime from the Fruit & Vegetables layer so that he can enhance the color of that specific object. Before he extracts it, however, he will create a copy of the original layer and make his extraction on the duplicate layer. Creating the duplicate layer ensures that the non-extracted objects will remain intact.

Steps

1. Click the **Layers tab** Layers next to the Channels tab Channels
   The Layers palette appears.

2. Make sure the **Fruit & Vegetables layer** is active, click the **Layers palette list arrow** , click **Duplicate Layer**, type **Lime** in the As text box, then click **OK**
   The new layer appears at the top of the Layers palette, and is now the active layer.

3. Click **Image** on the menu bar, then click **Extract**
   The Extract dialog box opens, displaying the images on the Lime layer, as shown in Figure G-6. This dialog box contains a unique set of extraction tools and a Zoom Tool to enlarge the area that you will extract.

4. Click the **Zoom Tool** in the Extract dialog box, then double-click the **center of the lime**
   The area containing the lime is magnified.

5. Click the **Edge Highlighter Tool** in the dialog box, double-click the **Brush Size text box** on the right side of the dialog box, then type **5**
   The Edge Highlighter Tool is used like a paintbrush to draw a border around the selection that should be extracted. A smaller brush size makes it easier to define a small area. When you click , the pointer changes to . You use to trace the edge of the object you want to extract. The border you create can overlap the edge of the grapefruit and the background.

Trouble?
When you define an area to be extracted with make sure you draw a closed boarder (a continuous line without gaps). Otherwise, when you click , you will fill the entire Photoshop window, rather than the border.

6. Drag around the perimeter of the lime, click the **Fill Tool** in the dialog box, then click the **center of the lime**
   The lime is surrounded by the highlighted border and filled in blue, as shown in Figure G-7. The highlight and fill colors can be changed using the Highlight and Fill list arrows in the Extract dialog box.

7. Click **Preview** in the upper-right corner of the Extract dialog box
   The highlighted lime appears on the layer with a transparent background.

Trouble?
The exact dimensions of your extracted object will differ.

8. Click **OK**, then click the **eye button** on the **Fruit & Vegetables layer** in the Layers palette
   The Fruit & Vegetables layer is no longer visible. The Lime layer contains only the extracted lime, as shown in Figure G-8.

QuickTip
The History palette does not record actions performed in the Extract dialog box.

9. Click the **Show/Hide layer button** on the **Fruit & Vegetables layer**, click **File** on the menu bar, then click **Save**

FIGURE G-6: Extract dialog box

Edge Highlighter Tool ──

Extraction tools ──

A lower value creates a smaller brush size

FIGURE G-7: Selection defined for extraction

── Preview button

── Click list arrow to change Highlight color

── Click list arrow to change Fill color

Filled selection ──

Highlighted selection ──

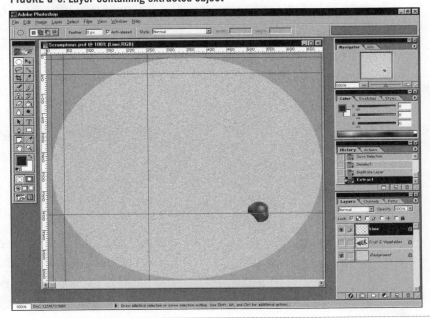

FIGURE G-8: Layer containing extracted object

Photoshop 6.0

Fixing a Blemish

As you gather images to work with in Photoshop, you may come across some that have defects, such as scratches or stains. Before rejecting such images, you should know that some image defects can be repaired using tools in Photoshop. While you cannot repair the original document that an image came from, you can touch up images with some creative effects. The **Clone Stamp Tool** can copy a sample (selection of pixels) in an image that can then be pasted on top of a blemish. The size of the sample taken with the Clone Stamp Tool depends on the brush tip size you choose in the Brushes pop-up palette. You can cover up a flaw in a document by using the Clone Stamp Tool to copy a similar, but undamaged, area of the document, then paste it over the damaged portion. Steve wants to fix a blemish on one of the tomatoes on the Fruit & Vegetables layer.

1. Click the **Fruit & Vegetables layer** in the Layers palette

2. Click the **Zoom Tool** 🔍, then click the **center of the far-left tomato** until the zoom factor is 200%
   The tomato and the blemish on it, are easier to see.

3. Click the **Clone Stamp Tool** 🖫 on the toolbox

4. Click the **Painting Brush list arrow** on the tool options bar, click the **third brush tip from the right in the first row** then click to close the Brushes pop-up palette
   The brush tip will collect a sample from part of the tomato that is not blemished, then cover the damaged part. Before you can correct the defect, you need to define, or sample, the area you want to copy.

   Trouble?
   The pop-up palette does not close unless you click the Painting Brush list arrow again.

5. Verify that the Opacity setting on the tool bar is 100%, then position ◯ at **45 H/410 V**, as shown in Figure G-10
   This is the area that will be sampled, then used to cover the blemish.

6. Press **[Alt] (Win)** or **[Option] (Mac)**, the pointer changes to 🖫, then click 🖫 at **45 H/410 V**
   The sample is collected and can be applied to the blemish.

   Trouble?
   If your brush size is too small, you may have to click more than once to cover a blemish.

7. Release **[Alt] (Win)** or **[Option] (Mac)**, position ◯ *directly* over the blemish, then click
   The sample covers the blemish, as shown in Figure G-11.

8. Click 🔍, press and hold **[Alt] (Win)** or **[Option] (Mac)**, click the **center of the tomato** until the zoom factor is 100%, then release **[Alt] (Win)** or **[Option] (Mac)**

9. Click **File** on the menu bar, then click **Save**

CLUES TO USE

Understanding actions

Many software programs include features that let you automate repetitive tasks. In Photoshop, these automated groups of commands are called actions. An **action** is a series of tasks that you record and save to play back later as a single command using the Play button ▶ in the Actions palette. The Actions tab, next to the History tab, shown in Figure G-9, can be clicked to display the Actions palette. You create, edit, and play actions using the VCR buttons, menu commands, and tools at the bottom of the Actions palette. For example, you can create an action that flattens a document.

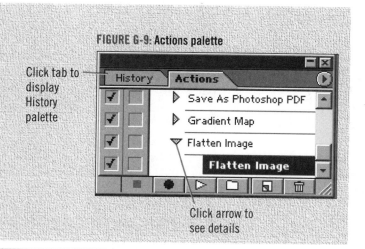

FIGURE G-9: Actions palette

Click tab to display History palette

Click arrow to see details

FIGURE G-10: Defining the area to be sampled

Clone Stamp Tool

Sample area   Area to be repaired

FIGURE G-11: Defect corrected with Clone Stamp Tool

Repaired area

Erasing Areas in an Image

As you learned in a previous lesson, the Extract command automatically discards the area of an image that is not highlighted with the Edge Highlighter Tool. While working in Photoshop, there may be instances when you want to simply erase an area *without* going through the extraction process. The **Background Eraser Tool** lets you selectively remove pixels from a document as you would use a pencil eraser to remove unwanted written marks. The erased areas become transparent, allowing pixels from other layers to appear in the document. Steve wants to erase the lime in the original layer, then modify the extracted image on the Lime layer. He begins by hiding the Lime layer so he can see only the lime on the Fruit & Vegetables layer.

Steps

1. Click the **eye button** 👁 on the **Lime layer** in the Layers palette, then click the **Fruit & Vegetables layer**
   With the Lime layer no longer visible, you will be able to see the effects of using the Background Eraser Tool.

2. Click the **Zoom Tool** 🔍, then click the **center of the lime** until the zoom factor is 200%

3. Click the **Eraser Tool** on the toolbox, then holding the mouse button until the tools list appears, click the **Background Eraser Tool**
   The pointer changes to the last brush tip used with this tool. You want to select a smaller brush tip. You can alternate between displaying , , and by clicking the active eraser tool, pressing and holding [Shift], pressing E, then releasing [Shift].

4. Click the **Painting Brush list arrow** on the tool options bar, click the **third brush tip from the left in the first row** in the Brushes pop-up palette, then click to close the palette
   Now you can begin erasing the lime.

5. Drag ⊕ over the lime until it is completely erased
   See Figure G-12. Each time you click ⊕, Photoshop creates a new entry in the History palette. As you drag ⊕, the foreground and background colors change each time the pointer moves over a different colored pixel.

6. Click the **Lime layer** in the Layers palette, click 🔍, press and hold **[Alt] (Win)** or **[Option] (Mac)**, click the **center of the lime** until the zoom factor is 100%, then release **[Alt] (Win)** or **[Option] (Mac)**
   Notice that when you click the Lime layer, the eye button returns automatically, displaying the contents of the Lime layer.

7. Click **Image** on the menu bar, point to **Adjust**, then click **Color Balance**
   The Color Balance dialog box opens.

8. Type the values **-14**, **45**, and **-40** in the Color Levels text boxes, as shown in Figure G-13, then click **OK**
   The green color of the lime appears more vibrant, as shown in Figure G-14.

9. Click **File** on the menu bar, then click **Save**

FIGURE G-12: Selection erased from layer

Erased area

FIGURE G-13: Color Balance dialog box

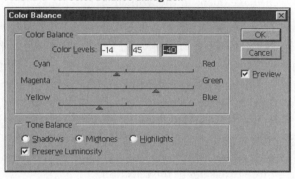

FIGURE G-14: Color balanced layer

Enhanced object

Using the Magic Eraser Tool

You can use the Magic Eraser Tool [icon] to erase areas in an image that have similar colored pixels. You can set the **tolerance**—how close a pixel color must be to another color in order to be erased with the tool. The lower the tolerance, the closer the color must be to the selection. You can also specify the **opacity** of the eraser strength. A 100% opacity erases pixels to complete transparency. To use the tool, click [icon] on the toolbox, then change the tolerance and opacity settings using the text boxes and list arrows on the tool options bar. Once you select [icon], the pointer changes to [icon]. Position [icon] over the pixels you want to erase, then click to erase pixels matching your criteria.

Photoshop 6.0

Photoshop 6.0

Making Specific Selections

You can drag an entire image, or a portion of an image, from one Photoshop document to another. If you want to drag just a portion of an image, you must select the part you want, then drag the selection into the current document. Photoshop provides several selection methods, including the Extract command and the **Magic Wand Tool**. The Magic Wand Tool lets you select pixels similar to those in a specific area of the document. Adjusting the **tolerance** (range of pixels) and **opacity** (percentage of transparency that allows the underlying layers to appear) defines how closely the pixels must match. Steve wants to select a flower from another Photoshop document and drag it into the Scrumptious file.

Steps

1. Open **Purple Fringed Gromwell.psd** from the drive and folder where your Project Files are stored
   The flower image opens in the work area.

2. Drag the **new window** to the lower-right portion of the screen, as shown in Figure G-15

3. Click the **Magic Wand Tool** on the toolbox, type **100** in the Tolerance text box on the tool options bar; if necessary, verify that the Contiguous check box is selected, then press **[Enter] (Win)** or **[Return] (Mac)** if you changed the Tolerance value
   Once you click , the pointer changes to . If the Contiguous check box is checked, only pixels touching the selection marquee will be selected.

QuickTip

You can change the opacity information by double-clicking the Opacity text box in the Layers palette.

4. Click the **document** at **50 H/200 V**
   White pixels within the image are selected. You can use the Select menu to select the inverse—those pixels *not* in the selection.

5. Click **Select** on the menu bar, then click **Inverse**
   The entire flower is selected and ready to be dragged to the Scrumptious document, as shown in Figure G-16.

QuickTip

You can drag a layer from one document into another document.

6. Position the pointer over one of the purple flower petals, press and hold **[Ctrl] (Win)** or **[Command] (Mac)**, when the pointer changes to , click-and-drag **the flower** into the Scrumptious document window, then release **[Ctrl] (Win)** or **[Command] (Mac)**
   The flower is copied to a new layer called Layer 1 in the Scrumptious document.

7. Click the **Move Tool** on the toolbox, then drag the **flower** to **250 H/50 V** using the snap-to-guide feature to position the object
   The flower is repositioned in the Scrumptious document.

8. Drag **Layer 1** beneath the Fruit & Vegetables layer
   The object in Layer 1 (the flower) is behind the Fruit & Vegetables layer, as shown in Figure G-17.

9. Click **File** on the menu bar, then click **Save**

Using the Lasso Tools

In addition to the Magic Wand Tool, you can also select an object on a layer using the Lasso Tool , the Polygonal Lasso Tool , and the Magnetic Lasso Tool . These tools are used like a pencil to draw a border around the image that you want to select. The Polygonal Lasso Tool requires that you click once to begin the first line segment of the border, then click again to finish the first segment of the border. To close the border, you click again at the starting point. You can use to create a selection that snaps to the edge of an object. As you drag around an object, a border forms that snaps to the strongest edge of the object.

FIGURE G-15: New document opened and repositioned

FIGURE G-16: Pixels selected in document

Selected pixels ———

FIGURE G-17: Selected object in existing document

Photoshop 6.0

Understanding Snapshots

The History palette records the last 20 tasks, or states, that you performed in Photoshop. As you learned in this unit, states can be deleted from the History palette to undo an unwanted action. When the History palette contains its maximum of 20 states, it starts deleting the oldest states to make room for new states. You can create a **snapshot**, a temporary copy of your document that contains the history states made to that point, so that you can work with more than one version of your document. You can create multiple snapshots in an image, and you can switch between snapshots as necessary. Steve reviews snapshot properties and considers how he can use this feature.

Details

Snapshot creation

You can create a snapshot using the **Create new snapshot button** in the History palette. Each time you click, the new snapshot appears in successive order at the top of the History palette. Snapshots are numbered consecutively. If you create the snapshot using in the History palette, you can rename the snapshot by double-clicking it, then typing a new name in the Name text box of the Rename Snapshot dialog box. You can also create a snapshot by clicking the History palette list arrow, then clicking New Snapshot. The New Snapshot dialog box opens, as shown in Figure G-18. Type a unique name in the Name text box, if necessary, then click OK.

A temporary solution

Although you can create multiple snapshots in one document while it is open, you cannot save the snapshot when you save and close the document.

Snapshot contents

You can create a snapshot based on the full document, merged layers, or the current layer. A snapshot of the full document includes all layers in the current document. A snapshot of merged layers combines all the layers in the current document on a single layer. A snapshot of the current layer includes only the active layer at the time that the snapshot command is given.

Switch between snapshots

Once you create multiple snapshots, as shown in Figure G-19, you can switch from snapshot to snapshot. Clicking a snapshot makes that snapshot—and all its history states—active.

Experiment with techniques

By switching between snapshots, you can experiment with different techniques and effects, such as filters and layer masks. You can see how certain techniques look when applied to images with different properties.

Snapshots act as a backup

If you take a snapshot *before* you apply a new technique, you can easily recover your work if you are dissatisfied with the results. The snapshot feature makes it easy to recover your work, and takes up considerably less disk space than saving several copies of the same file.

FIGURE G-18: New Snapshot dialog box

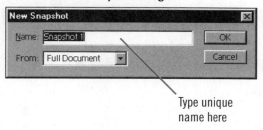

Type unique
name here

FIGURE G-19: Snapshots in History palette

Original
snapshot

New
snapshot

Creating a Multiple-Image Layout

Photoshop allows you to generate several types of multiple-image layouts. Multiple-image layouts are useful when you need to gather one or more Photoshop documents in a variety of sizes for a variety of uses. You can generate a single layout, known as **picture package**, which contains multiple sizes of a single document. The picture package option lets you choose from 20 possible layouts of the same document, and then places them in a single file. You can assemble a maximum of 30 thumbnail images in a specific folder, called a **contact sheet**. If the folder used to compile the contact sheet contains more than 30 files, Photoshop automatically creates new sheets so that all the documents appear. ▰▰▰ Steve wants to generate a picture package of the catalog cover, and create a contact sheet using files for various clients.

Steps

1. Click **File** on the menu bar, point to **Automate**, then click **Picture Package**
   The Picture Package dialog box opens, as shown in Figure G-20. You can choose the current document you are working on, or another Photoshop document on your computer, using the Choose button.

2. Click the **Use Frontmost Document check box**, click the **Layout list arrow**, click **(1) 5 × 7 (2) 2.5 × 3.5 (4) 2 × 2.5**, then click **OK**
   A series of actions takes place while the picture package command is in progress. The picture package is finished when the new file, called Picture Package, appears, as shown in Figure G-21.

   > **QuickTip**
   > Photoshop creates a temporary storage file (called Scrumptious copy) while it creates the picture package, then deletes the file when sheets consecutively.

3. Click **File** on the menu bar, click **Save**, click the **Save in list arrow (Win)** or the **Current file location list arrow (Mac)**, find the drive and folder where your Project Files are stored, accept the default name (Picture Package.psd), then click **Save**

4. Click **File** on the menu bar, point to **Automate**, then click **Contact Sheet II**
   The Contact Sheet II dialog box opens, as shown in Figure G-22.

   > **QuickTip**
   > Photoshop automatically numbers additional contact sheets consecutively.

5. Click **Choose**, locate the drive and folder containing your Project Files, click **OK (Win)** or **Choose (Mac)**, then click **OK** to close the Contact Sheet II dialog box
   All your Project Files are opened and placed in a new file called Contact Sheet-1.

6. Click **File** on the menu bar, click **Save**, click the **Save in list arrow (Win)** or the **Current file location list arrow (Mac),** find the drive and folder where your Project Files are stored, accept the default name (ContactSheet-1.psd), then click **Save**

7. Click **Window** on the menu bar, click **Scrumptious.psd**, click the **Type Tool** [T] on the toolbox, click the image at **40 H/590 V**, type your name, then click the **Move Tool** ▸⊕
   Your name appears in the lower-left corner of the image. You may have to resize or reposition the type to make it fit in the document.

8. Click **File** on the menu bar, then click **Save**

9. Print **one copy** of Scrumptious, then **Exit (Win)** or **Quit (Mac)** Photoshop—*do not save changes to Purple Fringed Gromwell.psd*

FIGURE G-20: Picture Package dialog box

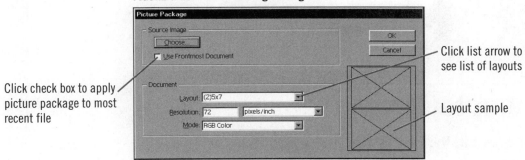

Click check box to apply picture package to most recent file

Click list arrow to see list of layouts

Layout sample

FIGURE G-21: Completed picture package

FIGURE G-22: Contact Sheet II dialog box

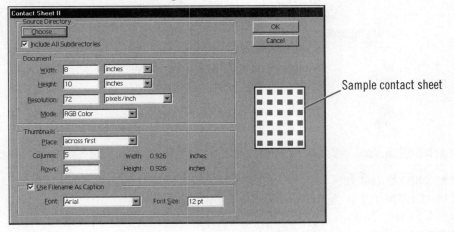

Sample contact sheet

CLUES TO USE

Creating a Web Photo Gallery

You can export graphic image files that will be used for a Web site by generating a Web Photo Gallery. A **Web Photo Gallery** contains a thumbnail index page of all files you choose. Create a Web Photo Gallery by clicking File on the menu bar, pointing to Automate, then clicking Web Photo Gallery. You can choose which files to include in the gallery by clicking the

Source button, and choose the gallery location by clicking the Destination button. Before you click OK to generate the Web Photo Gallery, you can customize the look of your Web Photo Gallery using the options under the Styles and Options list arrows. You can also choose a font and font size for the gallery, and name the photographer in the Photographer text box.

Photoshop 6.0

Practice

► Concepts Review

Label each element in the Photoshop window shown in Figure G-23.

FIGURE G-23

Match each button, tool, pointer, or phrase with the statement that describes its function.

7. **Background Eraser Tool**
8. **Contains snapshots**
9. **Magnetic Lasso Tool**
10. **Automates tasks**
11. **Magnetic Lasso pointer**
12. **Edge Highlighter Tool**

a. Actions
b. ![icon]
c. ![icon]
d. ![icon]
e. History palette
f. ![icon]

Select the best answer from the list of choices.

13. Which setting determines the closeness with which pixels must match?
    a. Tolerance
    b. Opacity
    c. Pixelocity
    d. Snapshot

14. Which tool do you click to play an action?
    a. [image]
    b. [image]
    c. [image]
    d. [image]

15. Which tool do you use to fix a blemish?
    a. [image]
    b. [image]
    c. [image]
    d. [image]

16. Which pointer is used to erase portions of an image?
    a. [image]
    b. [image]
    c. [image]
    d. [image]

17. Which feature do you use to isolate an object from a background?
    a. Channel
    b. Extract
    c. Scale
    d. Filter

18. Which tool do you use to erase areas based on pixel color?
    a. [image]
    b. [image]
    c. [image]
    d. [image]

19. Which of the following is *not* found in the Extract dialog box?
    a. [image]
    b. [image]
    c. [image]
    d. [image]

20. When erasing pixels, which palette do you use to change the size of a pointer?
    a. History
    b. Actions
    c. Brushes
    d. Channels

21. Which of the following is a collection of thumbnails generated from a folder of Photoshop documents?
    a. Web Photo Gallery
    b. Picture package
    c. Alpha channel
    d. Contact Sheet II

 # Skills Review

1. **Create an alpha channel.**
   a. Start Photoshop.
   b. Open PS G-2 from the drive and folder where your Project Files are stored, then save it as *Tool World*.
   c. Make sure the rulers appear, then enlarge the image to 150%.
   d. Click the Channels tab, if necessary, to show the Channels palette.
   e. Click the Rectangular Marquee Tool on the toolbox, then type 25 in the Feather text box on the tool options bar.
   f. Create a selection from 55 H/20 V to 450 H/270 V using the snap-to-guides feature and the guidelines to locate the coordinates.
   g. Click the Save selection as channel button in the Channels palette, then click the new channel, Alpha 1.
   h. Click Select on the menu bar, then click Deselect.
   i. Save your work.

2. **Extract an object.**
   a. Click the Layers tab to display the Layers palette.
   b. Click the Tools layer, then make a duplicate of the layer named Yellow Tape.
   c. Click the Yellow Tape layer.
   d. Click Image on the menu bar, then click Extract.
   e. Click the Zoom Tool in the Extract dialog box to enlarge the view of the roll of yellow tape.
   f. Click the Edge Highlighter Tool in the Extract dialog box, then change the brush size to 5.
   g. Draw a border around the roll of yellow tape.
   h. Click the Fill Tool in the dialog box to fill the highlighted area.
   i. Preview the extraction, then click OK.
   j. Save your work.

3. **Fix a blemish.**
   a. Click the Tools layer.
   b. Click the Clone Stamp Tool on the toolbox.
   c. Click the Painting Brush list arrow on the tool options bar, then click the third brush from the left in the first row.
   d. Sample the area to be *pasted* as 370 H/80 V by pressing [Alt] (Win) or [Option] (Mac) over the sample area (a grayed area).
   e. Click the red dot (at approximately 350 H/85 V).
   f. Save your work.

4. Erase areas in an image.

   a. Use the Zoom Tool to magnify the roll of yellow tape.

   b. If you do not see the Background Eraser Tool on the toolbox, click the Eraser Tool on the toolbox, hold the mouse button until the tools list appears, then click the Background Eraser Tool.

   c. Hide the Yellow Tape layer.

   d. Erase the roll of yellow tape.

   e. Make the Yellow Tape layer active.

   f. Use the Zoom Tool to restore the magnification to its original setting.

   g. Adjust the Color Balance settings on the Yellow Tape layer to +75, +25, and -80. (Click Image on the menu bar, point to Adjust, then click Color Balance.)

   h. Save your work.

5. Make specific selections.

   a. Click the Tools layer.

   b. Click the Magic Wand Tool, then set the Tolerance to 100.

   c. Click the image at 100 H/35 V.

   d. Click the Move Tool on the toolbox.

   e. Press Alt (Win) or Option (Mac), click the selection at 100 H/35 V, then drag the selection to 55 H/35 V.

   f. Deselect the object.

   g. Save your work.

6. Create a multiple-image layout.

   a. Click File on the menu bar, point to Automate, then click Picture Package.

   b. Use the frontmost document to create a (2) 4 × 5 (4) 2.5 × 3.5 picture package.

   c. Save the file with the name *Picture Package-2* in the drive and folder where your Project Files are stored.

   d. Click File on the menu bar, point to Automate, then click Contact Sheet II.

   e. Create a contact sheet using the ImageReady Animations that come with Photoshop. The location of this folder should be \Program Files\Adobe\Photoshop 6.0\ Samples\ImageReady Animations [Win] or Adobe Photoshop 6.0/Samples/ImageReady Animations [Mac].

   f. Save this file using the default naming scheme and the next available number.

   g. Click Window on the menu bar, then click Tool World.

   h. Show the Name and World of Tools type layers.

   i. Edit the Name layer to display only your name.

   j. Save your work, then print the Tool World document.

   k. Exit (Win) or Quit (Mac) Photoshop.

Independent Challenges

1. You decide to enter a photograph in the No-Holds-Barred Photo Contest, a local graphic arts competition. As the title implies, contestants can retouch an image in any way they desire. You are prepared to dazzle the judges with your Photoshop skills.

    a. Open PS G-3, then save it as *Contest Entry*.
    b. Create a duplicate of the Table and Chairs layer called Blue Bottle.
    c. Extract the blue bottle from the Blue Bottle layer.
    d. Erase the blue bottle from the Table and Chairs layer.
    e. Enhance the image on the Blue Bottle layer using the Color Balance or Brightness/Contrast adjustments.
    f. If you want, add additional filters to enhance the image.
    g. Create a picture package for the image using the (20) 2 × 2 layout.
    h. Save the picture package in the designated location as *Picture Package-3*.
    i. Display the Name layer, then modify it to include your name.
    j. Save and print the document.

2. A local landscape architecture business, Wild Blue Cosmos, hires you to create its first print ad. Business has been slow lately, and this ad is intended to generate new business. The architect likes the idea of a humorous ad, but she leaves the look and feel of the design up to you.

    a. Create a Photoshop file with the dimensions 300 pixels × 310 pixels, then save it as *Architect Ad*.
    b. Open at least two Photoshop images available to you.
    c. Select portions of each image using selection tools, then drag them to the Architect Ad document.
    d. Apply any filters, effects, or enhancements that you want.
    e. Create any text you think will enhance the image.
    f. Modify the Background layer, if necessary.
    g. Type your name in the lower-right corner of the document.
    h. Save and print the document.

3. The political climate in your community is right for you to run for mayor. Because your budget is small, you decide to use Photoshop to create your own campaign poster.

a. Locate a color photograph of yourself. Scan the image and save it in the drive and folder where your Project Files are stored.
b. Locate a color print of a dog or cat, or other image that will make you look trustworthy. Scan the image and save it in the designated location.
c. Create a Photoshop file with the dimensions 300 pixels × 310 pixels, then save it as *Campaign Poster*.
d. Select any part (or all) of the scanned image, then drag it into the Campaign Poster document.
e. Use filters, effects, or adjustments to make the images in the poster appealing.
f. Add any text, including your name and campaign slogan, that you feel will enhance the image.
g. Save and print the document.

4. You are hired to create an advertisement for a classic car restoration shop. You can use the Internet to locate royalty-free, downloadable artwork that you can insert in a Photoshop document and modify to suit your needs.

a. Connect to the Internet and go to Free Clip Images at *http://www.free-clip-images.com/main.html*.
b. Search the site for images of cars you want in your advertisement.
c. Create a 360 pixel × 290 pixel Photoshop document, then save it as *Auto Restoration*.
d. Create any necessary layers, including type layers with your name and the company name.
e. Insert the downloaded artwork in the Photoshop document, then modify it using erasing, extracting, or repairing skills.
f. Apply any additional techniques you feel are necessary to create a professional document.
g. Save and print the document.

Photoshop 6.0 | Practice

▶ Visual Workshop

Open PS G-4 from the drive and folder where your Project Files are stored, then save it as *Flower Study*. Use the skills you learned in this unit to modify the file so it looks like Figure G-24. Duplicate the Flowers layer and rename it Pansy. Extract the maroon pansy in the upper-right corner (on the new layer). (*Hint*: It may be easier to highlight the object if you use a brush size of 10.) Use the Background Eraser Tool to erase the pansy on the Flowers layer. Adjust the Color Balance on the Pansy layer using Midtones of +50, -30, and +20, and Highlights of -60, -40, and 0. Modify Brightness to +40 and Contrast to +10. Modify the Name layer to include your name. Save your work, then print the document.

FIGURE G-24

Photoshop 6.0

Unit **H**

Creating
Web Documents

The tools in Photoshop create attractive designs for print, multimedia, and Web pages. Adobe ImageReady 3.0—now an integral part of Photoshop—uses all of the features in Photoshop, as well as advanced capabilities for creating Web graphics. With ImageReady, you can create buttons, rollovers, and animations for Web sites. ⬟⬟⬟ Jesse Thompson is a Web Account Representative at Zenith Design. He completed the image design phase for an online shopping client, Flowers Forever. Jesse started working on the Flowers Forever home page. He will use features in Adobe ImageReady to create special effects that will call attention to this professionally designed Web site.

Understanding ImageReady

Photoshop features help you create graphics that can be used on Web pages. ImageReady offers you sophisticated Web-related capabilities, such as buttons, rollovers, and animation. These two programs combined provide all the tools you need to build an impressive and functional Web site. Although Photoshop 6.0 and ImageReady 3.0 are designed to work together, each program can be opened independently. Because both programs share features (such as the toolbox and palettes) and functionality, you can move between them without having to learn the characteristics of a new program. When Photoshop and ImageReady are both open, changes made in one program are automatically updated in the other program. Before he proceeds, Jesse reviews ImageReady capabilities.

 ### Common features and tools

Photoshop and ImageReady work areas share many common features, such as the toolbox and palettes. Both programs contain similar painting tools, and treat layers and type identically. Some features are available in both programs, but are located in slightly different areas.

In Photoshop, the History palette appears above the Layers palette. In ImageReady, the History palette appears as a tab in the Layers palette.

 ### Jump between programs

Using the Jump to ImageReady button ▣▣▣ shown in Figure H-1, you can easily switch between Photoshop and ImageReady. It is not necessary to exit one program before you jump to the other. The initial file stays open in the program where it originated (Photoshop or ImageReady), and the changes you make in one program are updated in the other program when you jump back.

QuickTip

You can control the automatic file update feature by clicking the Auto-update open documents check box in the General Preferences dialog box (Photoshop), or by clicking the Auto-Update Files check box in the General Preferences dialog box (ImageReady).

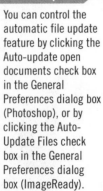 ### File updating

Each time you jump between Photoshop and ImageReady, the active program will automatically update the current file, ensuring that you always work with the most current version of the document.

 ### ImageReady features

ImageReady allows you to create impressive Web pages. The ImageReady work area, as shown in Figure H-2, looks similar to the Photoshop work area. In ImageReady, you can optimize images so that they take less time to download from Web pages. Using common Web formats, you can simultaneously view two or four optimized versions.

 ### Slices

A document created for use on a Web site can be divided into many smaller sections, or slices. **Slices** make it possible to assign special features—such as rollovers—to specific areas within a document.

 ### Rollovers

A **rollover** changes an object's appearance when the mouse pointer passes over (or clicks) a specific area of the document.

 ### Animations

Moving images, or **animations**, add dimension to your Web page. You can create an animation sequence on your Web page by changing the opacity of several images, and then adjusting the timing between their appearances.

FIGURE H-1: Document in Photoshop

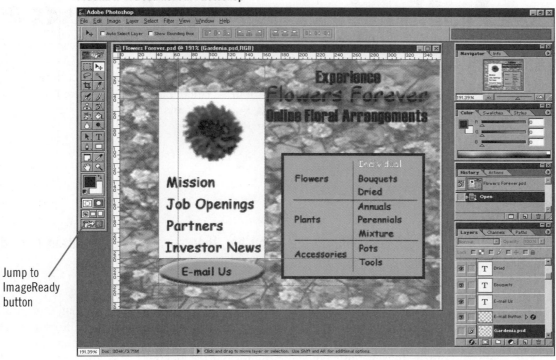

Jump to
ImageReady
button

FIGURE H-2: The ImageReady work area

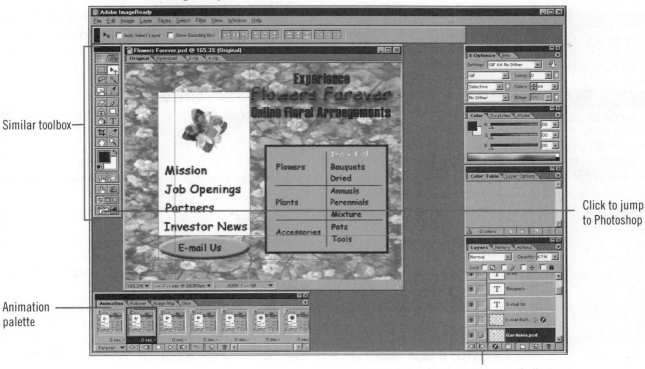

Similar toolbox

Animation
palette

Click to jump
to Photoshop

ImageReady palettes are similar to
Photoshop, but arranged differently

Photoshop 6.0

Optimizing an Image

A Web page with multiple graphics looks wonderful, but its overall effectiveness can be ruined if the graphics take too long to download. It's important to control the size of the images on your Web pages because download speeds vary. Photoshop and ImageReady support commonly used graphic formats that optimize graphic files without sacrificing image quality. You can compare optimized files before you convert them. ✎ Jesse wants to see how he can optimize a graphic image using both Photoshop and ImageReady.

Steps

1. Start Photoshop, click **File** on the menu bar, then open **Bachelor Button** from the drive and folder where your Project Files are stored

2. Click **File** on the menu bar, then click **Save for Web**
   The Save For Web dialog box opens. This dialog box has four tabs: Original, Optimized, 2-Up, and 4-Up. The Original view displays the graphic without any optimization. The Optimized, 2-Up, and 4-Up views display the graphic in its original format, as well as other file formats. You can change the file format by clicking one of the windows in the dialog box, then clicking the Optimize file format list arrow on the right. Before you decide which file format to choose, you can compare multiple versions of the current file using different formats.

   QuickTip
   Your active file format settings may vary.

3. Click the **4-Up tab**, click the **Settings list arrow**, then click **JPEG Medium**
   Four images appear in the dialog box. You can enlarge the images to examine them more closely.

   QuickTip
   Clicking any of the images in the dialog box will automatically enlarge all of the images.

4. Click the **Zoom Tool** 🔍 in the dialog box, then click the **image** in the upper-right corner
   The four images are enlarged, and the image in the upper-right corner is selected as the optimal format, as shown in Figure H-3. You can change the optimization settings by choosing a new file format.

5. Click the **Settings list arrow**, then click **GIF 128 Dithered**
   The images change to reflect the new file format, as shown in Figure H-4. You can close the dialog box without optimizing the image.

   QuickTip
   To optimize the file, click the desired image in the dialog box, then click OK. Enter a new name for the image in the Save Optimized As dialog box.

6. Click **Cancel** in the dialog box
   The Save For Web dialog box closes. You can also optimize a file in ImageReady by using a similar procedure.

7. Click the **Jump to ImageReady button** 🔁 on the toolbox
   Adobe ImageReady 3.0 opens.

8. Click 🔍, if necessary verify that the **Resize Windows to Fit check box** is selected, click the **image**, then click the **4-Up tab**
   Four enlarged images appear in the ImageReady window, as shown in Figure H-5. You can close the ImageReady window without optimizing the image.

9. **Exit (Win)** or **Quit (Mac)** ImageReady, then close the **Bachelor Button** document
   ImageReady is closed. Photoshop remains open, but the work area is empty.

FIGURE H-3: Save For Web dialog box (JPEG)

Click tabs to change visual arrangement

Optimal format is outlined

Click list arrow to see approximate download times

Click list arrow to change file format

FIGURE H-4: Save For Web dialog box (GIF)

FIGURE H-5: Document optimized in ImageReady

Click list arrow to change format

Optimal format is outlined

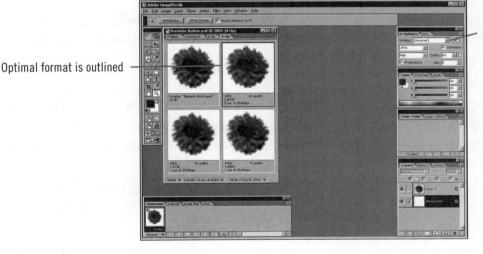

CLUES TO USE

Maintaining detail during file compression

Compressing graphic images is important because smaller files take less time to download. A file format that discards data during the compression process is referred to as **lossy**. To prevent data loss, you can use a higher-quality compression. During compression, the JPEG format, which supports 24-bit color, tends to lose detail. The GIF format, which uses 8-bit color, compresses solid color areas while maintaining detail. That is, GIF compression is **lossless** (no data is discarded). Nevertheless, because it uses 8-bit color, an image with 24-bit color can lose detail during compression. Both Photoshop and ImageReady offer the **lossy GIF** format, which compresses files while maintaining image quality.

Creating a Button

Most Web sites contain interactive features, such as buttons used to navigate to various pages and frames on the site. Buttons are also used to start an action on a Web page. Before you can create an action, you must first draw and stylize a button to which an action will be assigned. You can draw and stylize buttons in ImageReady. ~~~~~~ Jesse wants to create a button that users can click to send an e-mail message to the company.

Steps

1. Open **PS H-1** in Photoshop from the drive and folder where your Project Files are stored, then save the file as **Flowers Forever**

2. Click the **Default Foreground and Background Colors button** 🔲 on the toolbox, if necessary, then click the **Jump to ImageReady button** 📇 on the toolbox
   The foreground and background colors display the default settings, and Adobe ImageReady 3.0 opens.

> **QuickTip**
> Zoom controls in Photoshop and ImageReady operate independently.

3. Click **View** on the menu bar, click **Show Rulers**, click the **Zoom Tool** 🔍 on the toolbox, verify that the **Resize Windows to Fit check box** is selected, then click the **Fit on Screen button** `Fit on Screen` on the tool options bar
   The document fits in the window, as shown in Figure H-6. You can create a button on a new layer, then sample a color for it from within the document.

4. Click the **Individual layer** in the Layers palette, click the **Create a new layer button** 🔲 in the Layers palette, click the **Eyedropper Tool** 🖊 on the toolbox, then click the **blue background at 200 H/200 V**

5. Click the **Marquee Tool** 🔲 on the toolbox, hold the mouse button until the tools list appears, then click the **Elliptical Marquee Tool** ◯, drag 🔳 from **45 H/230 V to 160 H/265 V** (using the guides), double-click **Layer 1** in the Layers palette, type **E-mail Button** in the Name text box, then click **OK** to close the Layer Options dialog box
   The button area is selected, as shown in Figure H-7.

> **QuickTip**
> You may find that having both ImageReady and Photoshop open taxes your computer's resources. Be sure to save your files often.

6. Click the **Paint Bucket Tool** 🪣 on the toolbox, click the **selection at 100 H/250 V**, click the **Add a layer effect button** 🔘 in the Layers palette, then click **Bevel and Emboss**
   You can place type with a darker color on top of the button.

7. Click the **Type Tool** 🄣 on the toolbox, click the **Set the text color list arrow** on the tool options bar, click the **last color in the last row**, verify that **12 px** appears in the Set the font size text box, click 🄣 at **65 H/250 V**, then type **E-mail Us**
   The text appears on the button, as shown in Figure H-8.

8. Click **Select** on the menu bar, then click **Deselect Type**
   A blue line appears underneath text indicating that it can be edited.

9. Click **Select** on the menu bar, click **Deselect**, click **File** on the menu bar, then click **Save**

FIGURE H-6: Document fitting in window

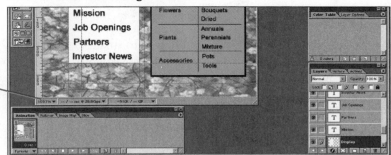

Click list arrow to modify
image display size

FIGURE H-7: Button selection

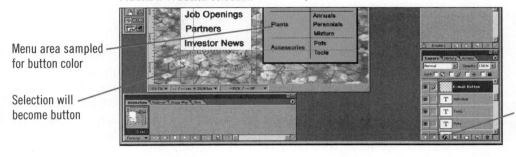

Menu area sampled
for button color

Selection will
become button

Add a layer effect
button

FIGURE H-8: Type added to button

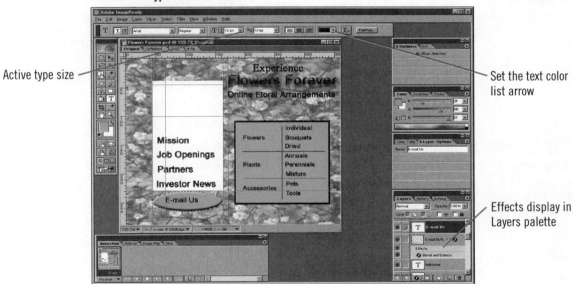

Active type size

Set the text color
list arrow

Effects display in
Layers palette

CLUES TO USE

Applying a style

You can make Web buttons much more visually interesting by applying a
style. A **style** is a pre-formatted design that includes effects, such as wood-
grain and shadows. You can choose from 18 pre-designed ImageReady
styles in the Styles palette, or you can create your own. Figure H-9 shows
the Styles palette. You can apply a style to a button by selecting it, then
double-clicking one of the style buttons in the Styles palette. The Style
Options dialog box opens and offers you additional choices based on the
particular style chosen. Click OK to close the Style Options dialog box.

FIGURE H-9: Styles palette

Photoshop 6.0

Using Slices

Using ImageReady, you can divide an image into smaller sections, or slices. A **slice** is a rectangular section of an image to which you can apply sophisticated features, such as rollovers and hyperlinks. You can create an unlimited number of slices in a document. A slice you create is a **user-slice**. When you create a user-slice, ImageReady automatically creates an **auto-slice**, which consists of the remaining area that is not defined by the user-slice. Photoshop documents for the Web are converted into Hypertext Markup Language (HTML) format. When a document is converted to HTML, each slice in the document becomes a cell in an HTML **table**, a rectangular object made up of columns and rows used for displaying data. ━━ Jesse wants to create slices over "Plants" and "Accessories" in the Forever Flowers document.

Steps

1. Click the **Slice Tool** 🖾 on the toolbox
   The pointer changes to ✂, the document fades, and any existing slices appear in the document, as shown in Figure H-10. User-slices are boxes outlined in blue with solid blue rectangles and numbers assigned to them in their upper-left corners. Your numbers may vary from those in the figures. You can create a slice by dragging ✂ on the area that you want to make into a slice.

   Trouble?
   Your slices may be numbered differently.

2. Using the guides, drag ✂ until it surrounds **Plants** *(from approximately 180 H/180 V to 260 H/190 V)*
   A new user-slice surrounds the type, as shown in Figure H-11.

3. Using the guides, drag ✂ until it surrounds **Accessories** *(from approximately 180 H/215 V to 260 H/230 V)*
   You can modify the dimensions of a slice using the Slice Select Tool 🖾.

4. Press and hold **[Shift]**, press **K**, then release **[Shift]**
   The Slice Select Tool 🖾 replaces the Slice Tool on the toolbox, and the pointer changes to ✂.

   QuickTip
   You can convert an auto-slice to a user-slice by selecting it, clicking Slices on the menu bar, then clicking Promote to User-slices.

5. Click the **Plants slice**
   Small yellow squares, called sizing handles, surround the slice. You can use the handles to change the dimensions of the slice. You want to enlarge the Plants slice.

6. Position the pointer over the **upper-middle handle** (at 220 H/180 V), then when it changes to ↕, drag ↕ to **175 V**
   The slice size increases. You can deselect the slice to better view the image.

7. Click **Select** on the menu bar, then click **Deselect Slices**
   The slice is no longer selected, as shown in Figure H-12.

8. Click **File** on the menu bar, then click **Save**

Assigning a URL

You can assign a URL (Web address) to slices in a document. When you click on the slice, you will engage a hyperlink that can jump to another Web site (or a page on your site), or initiate an action (such as creating an e-mail message). To assign a URL to a slice, click the Slice palette tab [Slice] to show the Slice palette. Click the slice to which you want to add the URL, then type the URL in the URL text box.

FIGURE H-10: Slices shown in ImageReady

Click the Slice Tool to display existing slices

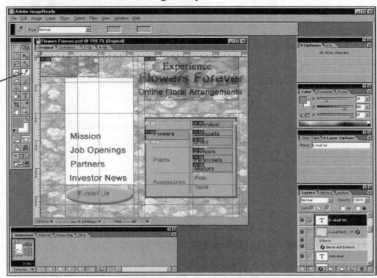

FIGURE H-11: New user-slice

New user-slice

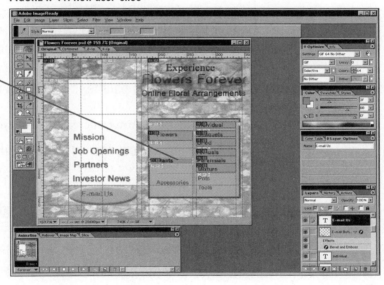

FIGURE H-12: Modified slices

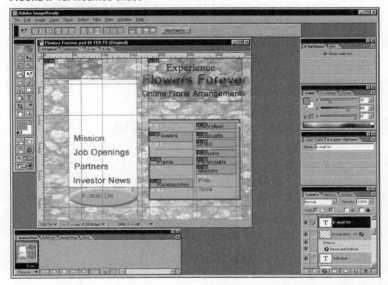

Creating a Rollover

Photoshop 6.0

Many Web pages feature actions that users initiate by moving the mouse pointer, or by clicking a specific area. You can create such an effect, called a **rollover**, with ImageReady. Rollovers can have many different appearances, called **states**, depending on the location of the mouse pointer. These states include Normal, Over, Down, Click, Out, Up, and None. You can change the appearance of each state using the tools in ImageReady, and you can control the layers on which they are placed. ✎ Jesse wants to create a rollover effect for the Individual category so that the type changes to white when the mouse rolls over it.

Steps

Trouble?

The Individual slice may be covered up by the blue rectangle. It is the first slice in the second column, as shown in Figure H-13.

1. Verify that the **Slice Select Tool** 🔖 is selected, then click the **Individual slice**

2. Click the **Rollover tab** 〔Rollover〕, as shown in Figure H-13
   The Rollover palette appears showing the Normal state. Other states can be added as necessary.

3. Click the **Creates new rollover state button** 🔲 in the Rollover palette
   The Over state appears in the Rollover palette, as shown in Figure H-13. You want to change the color of "Individual" to white in the Over state. First you'll need to copy "Individual" onto a new layer.

4. Click the **Individual layer** in the Layers palette, click **Select** on the menu bar, then click **Create Selection from Slice**
   A marquee surrounds the Individual slice. You can create a new layer from the selection.

5. Click **Layer** on the menu bar, point to **New**, then click **Layer via Copy**
   A new layer, Layer 1, appears above the Individual layer in the Layers palette. You can rename the layer.

6. Double-click **Layer 1** in the Layers palette, type **Individual Highlight** in the Name text box, then click **OK**
   You can hide the Individual type layer to make that layer look different during the rollover effect.

7. Click **Normal** in the Rollover palette, click the **eye button** 👁 on the **Individual Highlight layer** in the Layers palette
   You can modify the fill color of the Individual Highlight slice to give it a different appearance during the rollover.

8. Click **Over** in the Rollover palette, click **Edit** on the menu bar, click **Fill**, change the settings in the dialog box using Figure H-14 as a guide, then click **OK**
   The "Individual" text appears white, as does the Over state thumbnail in the Rollover palette, as shown in Figure H-15.

9. Click **File** on the menu bar, then click **Save**

Using Web-safe colors

The resolution of some monitors is limited by the number of colors they can display. In fact, exactly 216 colors are considered **Web-safe colors**. Using only these colors ensures that your images will be displayed without dithering. **Dithering** occurs when a Web browser attempts to display colors that are not included in its native color palette. If you select a non-Web color, an alert cube 🔲 appears in both the Color Picker dialog box and Color palette in Photoshop and ImageReady, respectively. You can limit your color selections to Web-safe colors by clicking the Only Web Colors check box in the Color Picker dialog box.

FIGURE H-13: New state in Rollover palette

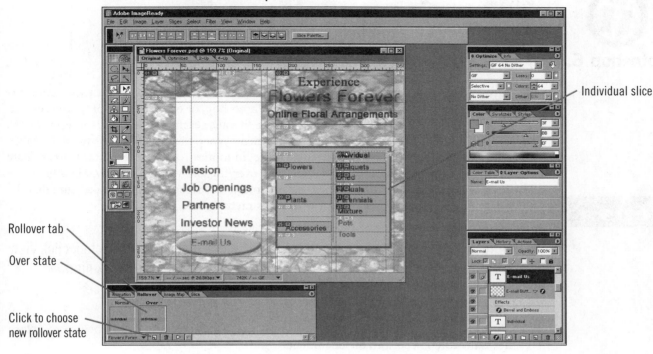

Individual slice

Rollover tab

Over state

Click to choose
new rollover state

FIGURE H-14: Fill dialog box

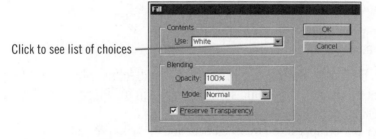

Click to see list of choices

FIGURE H-15: Completed rollover effect

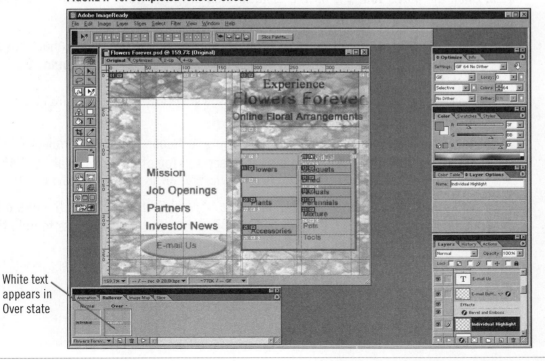

White text
appears in
Over state

Placing Files for Animation

Before you create an animation effect, you need to create the objects that will be used in the animation sequence. You can create such objects in Photoshop, or other graphic programs, or you can import them from a scanner or digital camera. Because each object appears intermittently, the objects can occupy the same spot in the document. When the document is shown on a Web page, the animated objects appear as a single object in motion. ✐ Jesse wants to animate three flowers each time the mouse pointer rolls over the Individual category. He adds three flower files that he created earlier to the Forever Flowers document. First, he makes sure that the Individual slice is selected, then hides the other distracting slices.

Steps

1. Verify that the **Individual slice** and the **Slice Select Tool** are selected, click **View** on the menu bar, point to **Show**, then click **Slices** to remove the check mark
   The slices disappear.

2. Verify that the **Over thumbnail** in the Rollover palette is selected
   When you animate a rollover state, you must select the appropriate state before you place the animation objects into the document.

3. Click the **Animation tab**
   The Animation palette appears, as shown in Figure H-16.

4. Click **File** on the menu bar, then click **Place**
   The File to Place dialog box opens.

5. Locate the **Bachelor Button** file in the drive and folder where your Project Files are stored, click **Open,** enter the same settings shown in the Place dialog box in Figure H-17, then click OK to close the Place dialog box
   The Bachelor Button appears on the document and in the thumbnail in the Animation palette.

6. Click the **Move Tool** on the toolbox, then drag the **flower** so that its upper-left corner is placed at **65 H/45 V** *(using the guides)*

7. Place the **Day Lily** file (found in the drive and folder where your Project Files are stored) into the document, then drag it directly on top of the **Bachelor Button** at **65 H/45 V**
   The Day Lily hides the Bachelor Button. Now you are ready to place the third object on top of the Day Lily.

8. Place the **Gardenia** file (found in the drive and folder where your Project Files are stored) into the document, then drag it directly on top of the Day Lily at **65 H/45 V**
   The Gardenia hides the Day Lily and the Bachelor Button, as shown in Figure H-18.

9. Click the **Rollover tab**, click the **Normal thumbnail**, click the **eye button** on the Gardenia.psd, Day Lily.psd, and Bachelor Button.psd layers to hide them, click the **Over thumbnail**, click **File** on the menu bar, then click **Save**
   Hiding the three flower layers in the Normal thumbnail prevents them from appearing during the Normal state.

FIGURE H-16: Animation palette

White type indicates rollover effect

Frames used in animation appear here

Animation palette

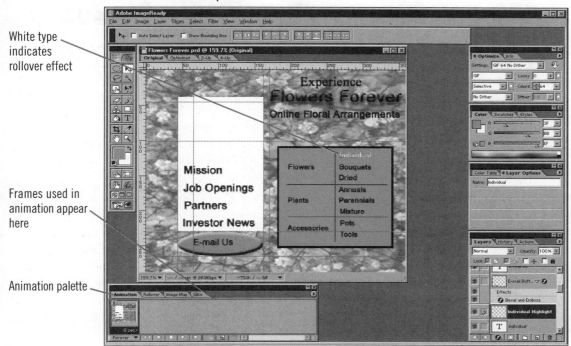

FIGURE H-17: Place dialog box

Your location may differ

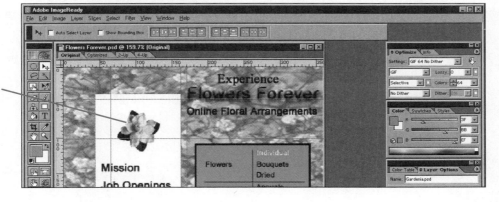

FIGURE H-18: Objects placed in document

Gardenia hides the other animation objects

CLUES TO USE

Saving a file for the Web

To use a Photoshop file on the Web, you must first convert it to HTML. Photoshop converts the information in your file to HTML, then stores it on the Clipboard. You can convert all of the slices in ImageReady to HTML by clicking Edit on the menu bar, pointing to Copy HTML Code, then clicking For All Slices. To insert the code into an HTML file, open a Web document in your favorite HTML editor, position the pointer where the copied code should appear, click Edit on the menu bar, then click Paste.

Creating Animation

Once you place objects that you want to animate in a document, you can then use the Animation palette to set up your animated sequence. The Animation palette contains frames that display a thumbnail of the objects that should appear during an animation sequence. You can use the Layers palette to hide and show layers that should appear in each frame. Each frame is a duplicate of the first frame. You can use play and stop buttons in the Animation palette to view your animation, and make changes, if necessary. ◄▬▬ Jesse is ready to animate the three flower objects he placed into the Forever Flowers document. He duplicates the first frame twice so that he has three frames, one for each flower to appear in during the animation.

Steps 1 2 3 4

1. Click the **Duplicates current frame button** 🔲 in the Animation palette
   An identical frame, Frame 2, appears in the Animation palette, as shown in Figure H-19. Each duplicate frame in the Animation palette will display one of the placed flower objects. You can hide layers that you do not wish to be visible in a particular frame.

> **QuickTip**
>
> You can adjust the size of the thumbnails by clicking the Animation palette list arrow, clicking Palette Options, then clicking a Thumbnail Size option button in the Animation Palette Options dialog box.

2. Click the **eye button** 👁, on the Gardenia.psd layer, then click 👁 on the Bachelor Button.psd layer in the Layers palette
   The Day Lily object appears, and the Bachelor Button and Gardenia objects are hidden, as shown in Figure H-20.

3. Click 🔲 in the Animation palette again to create a third frame
   Frame 3 appears in the Animation palette.

4. Click 👁 on the Day Lily.psd layer, then click the **Show/Hide layer button** ⬜ on the **Bachelor Button.psd layer** in the Layers palette to show the Bachelor Button in this frame
   The Bachelor Button layer appears in Frame 3.

> **QuickTip**
>
> The buttons controlling the animation resemble those found on a VCR.

5. Click **Frame 1** in the Animation palette, click 👁 on the Day Lily.psd layer and the Bachelor Button.psd layer in the Layers palette to hide these two flowers in Frame 1
   Each flower appears in a separate frame in the Animation palette, as shown in Figure H-21.

6. Click the **Plays animation button** ▶ in the Animation palette
   The animation appears in the document, and the frames in the Animation palette are highlighted consecutively, and loop until you click the Stops animation button.

7. Click the **Stops animation button** ⬛ in the Animation palette
   The animation stops in the active frame that was last played.

8. Click **File** on the menu bar, then click **Save**

Creating an image map

You can select an area within a document to use as a hyperlink. Each area, or **hotspot**, is assigned a URL. When you click it, the browser jumps to a different Web site. Multiple hotspots make up an **image map**, which is similar to a slice, in that you can link a particular area to a URL. Unlike a slice, an image map can be a circle, rectangle, or polygon. You can create an image map in ImageReady by selecting the Rectangle Image Map Tool 🔲, the Circle Image Map Tool 🔲, or the Polygon Image Map Tool 🔲 from the toolbox. Use ⁻⁺⁻ to create a selection you want as a hotspot. When the selection is drawn, the Image Map palette automatically appears, and you can type a Web address in the URL text box. When you preview the page in your browser, and place 🖑 over the hotspot, the URL will appear on the status bar.

FIGURE H-19: Duplicate frame in Animation palette

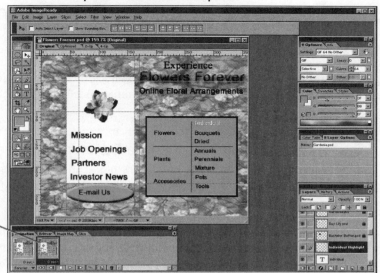

Duplicate frame

FIGURE H-20: Day Lily object appears in frame

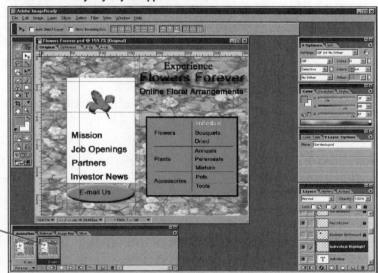

Visible object appears
in frame

FIGURE H-21: Each placed object in a frame

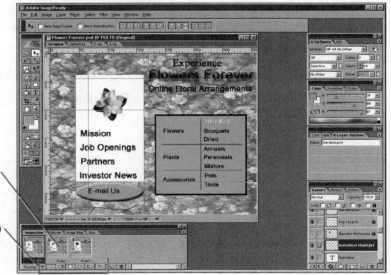

Each flower shown
in a frame

Use VCR buttons to
play animation

Photoshop 6.0

Photoshop 6.0

Enhancing Animation

You can enhance animation by adding an effect that makes frames appear to blend into one another. This effect, called **tweening**, adds frames to the document, and gives the animation a more fluid appearance. Tweening involves selecting multiple frames, then inserting transitional frames between them. Jesse wants to tween the flower animation to give it a smoother appearance.

Steps

1. Click **View** on the menu bar, click **Hide Rulers** if necessary, click **Frame 1** in the Animation palette if necessary, press and hold **[Shift]**, then click **Frame 2**
   The rulers are no longer visible, and Frames 1 and 2 are selected. The Tweens animation frames button is located to the right of the VCR buttons in the Animation palette.

2. Click the **Tweens animation frames button** in the Animation palette
   The Tween dialog box opens. This dialog box determines which frames to tween, the number of additional frames, and whether to tween all layers, or just the selected layers.

   > **QuickTip**
   > Depending on previous settings, you may not need to modify the settings in the Tween dialog box.

3. Using Figure H-22, make sure you have the same settings in your Tween dialog box, then click **OK**
   Two additional frames appear after Frame 1 in the Animation palette, as shown in Figure H-23. You can use the same technique to tween the remaining original frames, Frame 4 and Frame 5.

   > **QuickTip**
   > You can accept the current settings in the Tween dialog box because they did not change since you last set them.

4. Click **Frame 4** in the Animation palette, press and hold **[Shift]**, click **Frame 5**, click , then click **OK** in the Tween dialog box
   Two new frames appear between the previously selected frames. The Animation palette contains seven frames, as shown in Figure H-24. The tweening process is complete; you can now play the animation.

5. Click the **Plays animation button** in the Animation palette, then click the **Stops animation button** in the Animation palette when you finish viewing the animation
   The animation stops. The active frame is the one that was playing when you clicked . You can also view the animation in a Web browser.

6. Click the **Preview in Default Browser button** or on the toolbox
   Your browser opens and shows the Forever Flowers document as a static image. Position the mouse pointer over "Individual." The pointer becomes , the type changes color, and the animation begins to play. Figure H-25 shows the animation in Internet Explorer. When you finish viewing the animation, close the browser.

   > **QuickTip**
   > Photoshop added the browsers on your computer to the Preview In menu choices during installation.

7. **Close (Win)** or **Quit (Mac)** your Web browser, click **File** on the menu bar, click **Save**, then **Exit (Win)** or **Quit (Mac)** ImageReady

8. Type your name in the lower-left corner of the document, then click the Move Tool

9. Save your work, **print** the document, then **Exit (Win)** or **Quit (Mac)** Photoshop

Setting animation delays

You can customize the time delay between frames. One frame can appear for a set time before the animation advances to the next frame. You can choose whole or partial seconds for the delay period. You can set the delay time by clicking the Selects frame delay time list arrow **0 sec.** below the active frame. When the list appears, click a delay time from the list. You can set a delay for an individual frame, or you can select multiple frames and simultaneously set the delays. For an accurate preview of the delay times, preview the animation in your browser. The preview will vary based on many factors, such as your computer's memory and processor speed.

FIGURE H-22: Tween dialog box

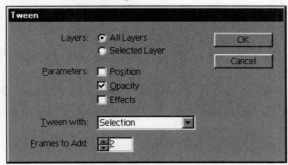

FIGURE H-23: Frames inserted during tweening

Frames added during tweening

FIGURE H-24: Seven frames in the Animation palette

Original frames

FIGURE H-25: Animation displayed in browser

Your browser may look different

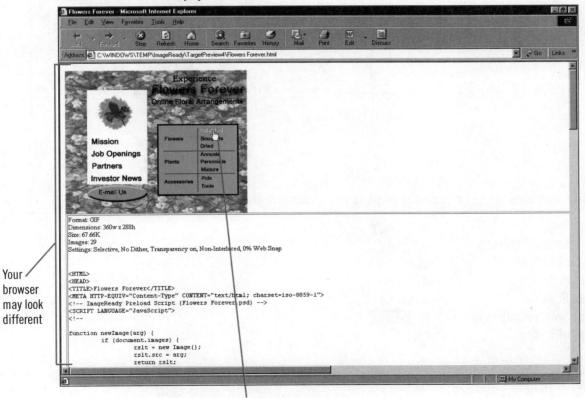

Animation begins when pointer is placed over type

Photoshop 6.0

Practice

▶ Concepts Review

Label each button or element in the Photoshop window shown in Figure H-26.

FIGURE H-26

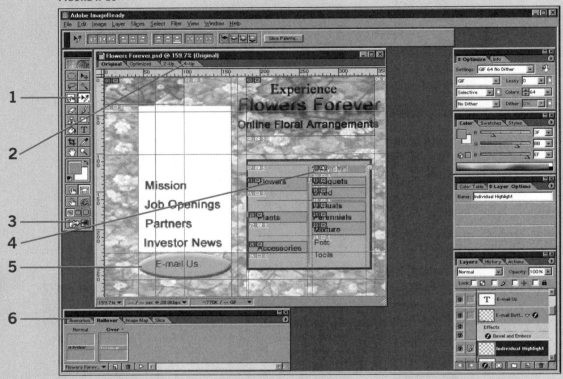

Match each button, tool, or pointer with the statement that describes its function.

7. Moves object   a.
8. Blends animation frames   b.
9. Adds effect to layer   c.
10. Sets frame delay   d.
11. Creates slices   e.
12. Jumps between Photoshop and ImageReady   f. 0 sec.

Select the best answer from the list of choices.

13. Which feature consists of smaller sections within a document?
    a. Frame
    b. Slice
    c. Rollover
    d. Selection

14. Which menu is used to see an optimized image in ImageReady?
    a. File
    b. Edit
    c. Slices
    d. No menu is needed.

15. Which button is used to stop an animation?
    a.
    b.
    c.
    d.

16. What do you call the process of adding transitional frames to animation?
    a. Slicing
    b. Transitionalizing
    c. Betweening
    d. Tweening

17. Which button is used to modify the shape of a slice?
    a.
    b.
    c.
    d.

18. Which palette is used to assign a URL to a slice?
    a. Layers
    b. Slice
    c. Rollover
    d. Animation

19. What is the name of the effect that occurs when an object's appearance changes after the pointer is positioned over it?
    a. Animation
    b. Smooth
    c. Delay
    d. Rollover

Photoshop 6.0

20. What occurs when a Web browser displays colors not included in its native palette?
    a. Wandering
    b. Dithering
    c. Compensating
    d. Drifting

21. Areas in an image map that are assigned a URL are known as
    a. Maplets.
    b. HotImages.
    c. Hotspots.
    d. Spotties.

▶ Skills Review

1. **Optimize an image.**
    a. Start Photoshop.
    b. Open Photoshop-1 from the drive and folder where your Project Files are stored.
    c. Click File on the menu bar, then click Save for Web.
    d. Click the 4-Up tab.
    e. Change the settings of the original image to GIF 64 Dithered.
    f. Click the Cancel button in the Save For Web dialog box.
    g. Jump to ImageReady.
    h. Zoom into the image.
    i. Click the 4-Up tab.
    j. Change the settings to JPEG High.
    k. Exit (Win) or Quit (Mac) ImageReady without saving your changes.
    l. Close the Photoshop-1 document, *but leave the Photoshop program open.*

2. **Create a button.**
    a. Open PS H-2, then save it as *Academia Online*.
    b. Set the background and foreground colors to the default.
    c. Jump to ImageReady.
    d. Fit the document to the screen.
    e. Click the Adobe Pagemaker layer, then use the Layers palette to create a new layer.
    f. Display the rulers, click the Slice Tool, then hide the slices if necessary.
    g. Use the Eyedropper Tool to sample the blue type color.
    h. Activate the Elliptical Marquee Tool, then draw a shape from 230 H/80 V to 350 H/125 V.
    i. Click the Paint Bucket Tool, then click the selection.
    j. Apply the Bevel and Emboss effect to the selection.
    k. Switch the foreground and background colors.
    l. Select the Type Tool.
    m. Click the document at 250 H/105 V, then type **Send Info** (using a 15 px Arial font).
    n. Deselect the type and the button object, then save your work.

3. Use slices.

a. Activate the Slice Tool.

b. Draw a slice from 0 H/155V to 180 H/175 V.

c. Draw a slice from 0 H/175 V to 180 H/200 V.

d. Draw a slice from 0 H/200 V to 180 H/225 V.

e. Draw a slice from 0 H/225 V to 180 H/250 V.

f. Save your work.

4. Create a rollover.

a. Click the Slice Select Tool, then select the Adobe Photoshop slice.

b. Click the Rollover tab.

c. Create a new rollover state.

d. Select the Adobe Photoshop layer in the Layers palette, then create a selection from a slice.

e. Create a new layer via copy (called *Photoshop Highlight*) based on the active layer.

f. Click the Normal state in the Rollover palette, then hide the Photoshop Highlight layer.

g. Click the Over state in the Rollover palette, then use the Fill command on the Edit menu to create black contents on rollover. (Make sure the Preserve Transparency check box is selected.)

h. Save your work.

5. Place files for animation.

a. Verify that the Adobe Photoshop layer and the Over frame are selected.

b. Click the Animation tab.

c. Hide the slices in the document.

d. Place Photoshop-1 in the document from the drive and folder where your Project Files are stored.

e. Click the Move Tool, then drag the object so its upper-left corner is at 240 H/175 V.

f. Place the Photoshop-2 object directly on top of the Photoshop-1 object.

g. Place the Photoshop-3 object directly on top of the Photoshop-2 object.

h. Select the Normal thumbnail in the Rollover palette, then hide the Photoshop-1, Photoshop-2, and Photoshop-3 layers.

i. Select the Over thumbnail in the Rollover palette.

j. Save your work.

6. Create animation.

a. Duplicate the current frame in the Animation palette.

b. Make sure the duplicate frame is active, then use the eye button to hide the Photoshop-1 and Photoshop-3 layers.

c. Duplicate the current frame in the Animation palette, then make sure only Photoshop-3 is visible in Frame 3.

d. Activate Frame 1, then make sure only Photoshop-1 appears.

e. Use the VCR buttons to play and stop the animation.

f. Save your work.

Photoshop 6.0

7. Enhance animation.

   a. Hide the rulers.

   b. Select Frame 1 and Frame 2.

   c. Click the Tweens animation frames button in the Animation palette, then accept the current settings.

   d. Select Frame 4 and Frame 5, click the Animation palette list arrow, click Tween, then accept the current settings.

   e. Use the VCR buttons to play and stop the animation.

   f. Type your name in the lower-right corner of the document.

   g. Click Save, Exit (Win) or Quit (Mac) ImageReady.

   h. Print the document in Photoshop.

   i. Exit (Win) or Quit (Mac) Photoshop.

▶ Independent Challenges

1. The online auction site, *youcanhaveit.com*, hires you to design its Web site. They want you to include animations and rollovers on the home page.

   a. Open PS H-3, then save it as *Online Auction*.

   b. Locate and open at least three other image files on your computer. Switch to ImageReady, then create slices for each of the online categories (antiques, automobiles, books, and computers).

   c. Place each object in the image.

   d. Create a rollover effect for each category.

   e. Use the placed objects to create an animation for one category.

   f. Tween the animation.

   g. Save the image, then jump back to Photoshop.

   h. Type your name in the lower-left corner of the document.

   i. Save and print the document.

2. Your local bookstore, The Book Nook, needs a new Web site. Your first task is to redesign their home page.

   a. Create a Photoshop document with the dimensions 360 pixels × 290 pixels, then save it as *Book Nook*.

   b. Create type layers, including the store name, your name, and the following book categories: Computers, Novels, History, Social Issues, and Cooking.

   c. Create slices in the image where appropriate.

   d. Create a rollover effect for each category.

   e. Type your name on the document.

   f. Save and print the document.

   g. Save a flattened copy of the document using the default naming scheme.

3. You are hired by your state's Motor Vehicle Division to make its Web site more exciting. The MVD wants to sponsor a contest for the most realistic license photo. This event is quite an undertaking for the MVD, and it needs your help.

    a. Locate and scan at least three driver's license photographs. (You can use your own.) Save the scanned images in the drive and folder where your Project Files are stored.

b. Create a Photoshop document with the dimensions 360 pixels × 290 pixels, then save it as *MVD Contest*.

c. Create type layers that describe the contest. Apply necessary formatting to the type layers.

d. Use ImageReady to create an animation using the scanned images.

e. Use tweening in the animation.

f. If necessary, apply enhancing effects to layers.

g. Exit (Win) or Quit (Mac) ImageReady.

h. Type your name in the lower-right corner of the document.

i. Save and print the document.

4. Your experience with Photoshop inspires you to create your own Web site, advertising your free-lance design services. It should highlight your skills, and give prospective clients a sense of your talents. You can download many images and buttons from the Internet to use for your project.

    a. Connect to the Internet and go to the All Clip Art Site at *http://www.allclipartsite.com*.

b. Download at least one button (you can download more, if necessary) for hyperlinks on the Web site.

c. Create a Photoshop document called *Webmaster* with the dimensions 360 pixels × 290 pixels.

d. Create any necessary layers, including a type layer that contains your name. (*Hint:* Type layers should emphasize your Photoshop skills.)

e. Use ImageReady to create any necessary slices.

f. Insert the downloaded button(s) in the Webmaster document.

g. Create type layers for the button text. (You can create URLs for the hyperlinks later.)

h. Save and print the document.

Photoshop 6.0

Photoshop 6.0 | *Practice*

► Visual Workshop

Open PS H-4 from the drive and folder where your Project Files are stored and save it as *Secaucus Online*. Use the skills you learned in this unit to modify the file so it looks like Figure H-27. Jump to ImageReady, then create the effects shown in the figure. Add your name to the document. Use black for the contents of the Fill Color in the Over frame. Save your work in ImageReady, then Exit (Win) or Quit (Mac) ImageReady, save your work, then print the document.

FIGURE H-27

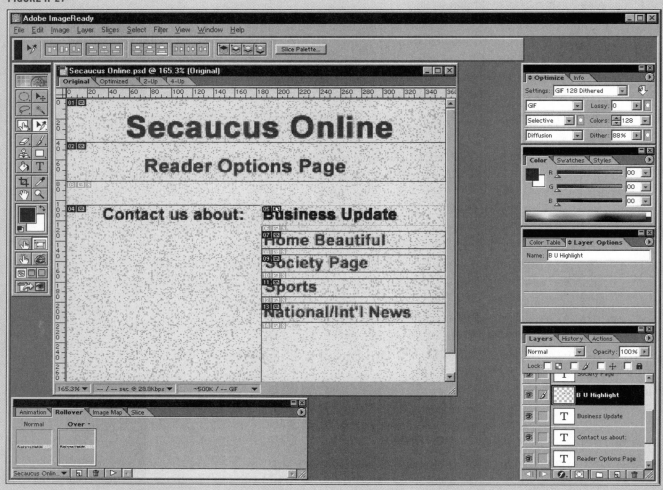

Appendix

Objectives

► **Calibrate a monitor**
► **Set preferences**
► **Select objects**
► **Use measurement tools**
► **Use plug-ins**
► **Understanding print options**
► **Acquire images**
► **Review keyboard shortcuts**

With a basic understanding of Photoshop concepts, you can create professional-looking images. By modifying settings within the program, you can fine-tune your working environment, as well as your documents. This appendix provides a handy reference for modifications, such as calibrating a monitor, setting preferences, learning keyboard shortcuts, and using plug-ins.

Photoshop 6.0

Calibrating a Monitor

By properly adjusting your monitor, you can ensure that printed colors will match the colors shown on your monitor. The Photoshop **Adobe Gamma utility** calibrates several settings, including the monitor's contrast and brightness, and color balance. This utility saves the new calibration settings as an International Color Consortium (ICC) profile on your computer. ICC standards are used to standardize colors across platforms, programs, and devices, such as other monitors.

Details

QuickTip

Make sure that your monitor has been on for at least one hour *before* you begin calibration to ensure accurate color display.

First-time use

When your computer first starts Photoshop, you may see a warning box recommending that you calibrate your monitor. During this process, your monitor and the Photoshop color conversion settings will be calibrated to compensate for factors that affect on-screen and printed colors.

Calibrating monitors

You can calibrate your monitor at any time using the Adobe Gamma utility program. To open the Adobe Gamma utility, click **Start** on the taskbar, point to **Settings**, click **Control Panel**, then double-click **Adobe Gamma (Win)**; or, click the **Apple menu**, point to **Control Panel**, then click **Adobe Gamma (Mac)**. The Adobe Gamma dialog box opens. Click the **Step By Step (Wizard) option button (Win)** or **Step By Step (Assistant) option button (Mac)** to use a series of helpful dialog boxes. Figure AP-1 shows the Adobe Gamma dialog box with the Step By Step (Wizard) option button selected. Click **Next** after making your selection. Continue making dialog box selections until the Wizard (Win) or Assistant (Mac) is complete.

If you are using Microsoft Windows Millennium Edition (Windows ME), click **view all Control Panel options** in the Control Panel dialog box to see the Adobe Gamma control panel icon. You may receive a message that reads "To run this program you must set your monitor to thousands of colors." If so, click **OK**, and the Adobe Gamma dialog box opens.

QuickTip

You can recalibrate the Color Management settings each time you change printers.

ICC profiles

The Adobe Gamma Wizard dialog box is the starting point for calibrating your monitor. You can use it to create different color profiles, or to modify your current profile using a Wizard (Win) or Assistant (Mac). Photoshop uses an ICC profile to describe monitor colors. A Color Management Module interprets the ICC profile and incorporates it into your documents. To use this automated process, click the **Step By Step** option button, then click **Next**. A series of dialog boxes guides you through the calibration process.

Macintosh

The monitor calibration tool used is called the Adobe Gamma *Assistant*.

Adobe Gamma Wizard

The third Adobe Gamma Wizard screen, shown in Figure AP-2, optimizes the brightness and contrast controls. Click **Next** to proceed to the next dialog box. This fourth Adobe Gamma Wizard screen identifies the phosphors setting used by your monitor. This setting controls the display of red, green, and blue phosphors. Click **Next** to proceed to the next dialog box. The fifth Adobe Gamma Wizard dialog box, shown in Figure AP-3, determines the brightness of the midtones. This dialog box determines if your monitor uses a warm or cool white. Click **Next** to proceed to the next dialog box. Once you answer all the wizard questions, click **Finish**. Your monitor will be calibrated according to your specifications.

FIGURE AP-1: Adobe Gamma dialog box

Calibration versions —

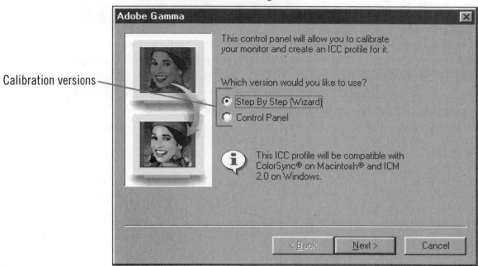

FIGURE AP-2: Adobe Gamma Wizard dialog box 3

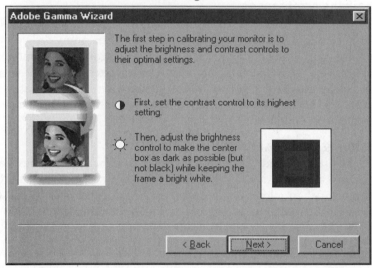

FIGURE AP-3: Adobe Gamma Wizard dialog box 5

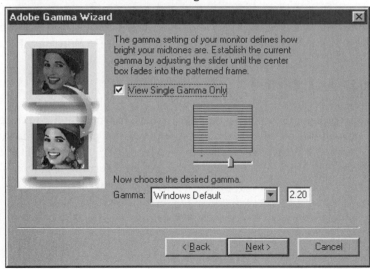

Photoshop 6.0

Setting Preferences

As you become more comfortable working in Photoshop, you may want to adjust some of the default settings. Instead of changing the settings each time you start the program, you can customize Photoshop with your commonly used settings to work more efficiently. To apply preferences to an individual file, open the file, then change the preference settings, as necessary. To change preferences globally, set preferences when no files are open.

Details

Preference topics

Preferences are stored in a specific folder on your computer. They include settings for the general display, separation setup, calibration options, display, and tools. You can also customize settings for ruler units and file formats.

QuickTip

You can access all of the categories from the Preferences list arrow.

Modifying preferences

You can modify preferences by using a command on the File menu. To modify Photoshop preference settings, click **Edit** on the menu bar, then point to **Preferences**. You can click the **General** category or one of seven preference categories. The Preferences dialog box opens and displays options related to the preference you selected. Figure AP-4 shows the Preferences dialog box for the General category. Once you make your modifications, click **OK**. Before you modify preferences on a computer that does not belong to you, check the policies or guidelines of your institution or company.

QuickTip

Palette locations may change when the Photoshop program window is resized.

Restoring default settings

You can use the Window menu to restore default location settings. To restore the default palette locations, click **Window** on the menu bar, then click **Reset Palette Locations**. The default location of the toolbox is the upper-left edge of the work area. The default location of the palettes is the right edge of the work area. To reset the default palette locations in ImageReady, click **Window** on the menu bar, point to **Arrange**, then click **Reset Palettes**.

Saving files

When saving a file, you can select optional viewing features that will apply the next time you open the file. One option is a thumbnail image preview that appears in the Open dialog box when you highlight the file. You can view a thumbnail of the document *before* you open it. The thumbnails let you see whether you have selected the correct file *without* opening it. In Macintosh, you also have the option of saving a desktop icon. You can append a three-character file extension to the file name, which is a necessity in Windows. Figure AP-5 shows the options for the Saving Files Preferences.

Displays and Cursors

You can use the Display & Cursors Preferences options to change Photoshop color selection. Image colors are stored in a color palette determined by the file's color mode and your monitor's capabilities. Dithering occurs when the color palette exceeds the monitor's range. You can use Display & Cursors settings, shown in Figure AP-6, to control the color palette and dithering. You can also use the Preferences dialog box to determine a pointer's default appearance and its hotspot. A pointer's **hotspot** is the area on the image that causes the pointer to react. Once you modify options in the Preferences dialog box, click **OK**.

FIGURE AP-4: General Preferences dialog box

Click list arrow to select other Preferences categories

Click for tools to return to default locations

Click to move between category dialog boxes

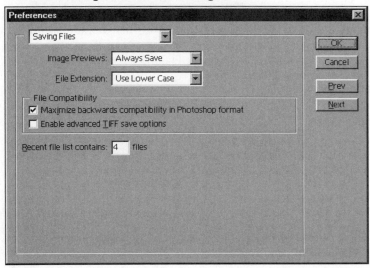

FIGURE AP-5: Saving Files Preferences dialog box

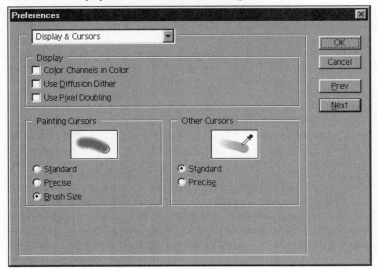

FIGURE AP-6: Display & Cursors Preferences dialog box

Selecting Objects

Photoshop 6.0

Accurately selecting objects is an important image-editing skill. Photoshop provides several tools to ensure that you select the precise object or area you want. You can select areas in an image by clicking and dragging a Marquee or Lasso Tool, or by targeting a specific color or range of colors.

Details

QuickTip

The Crop Tool ⛏ trims a selection.

Marquee Tools

The **Marquee Tools** ⬚, ◯, ⠿, and ⊞ on the toolbox are used to select areas in a document. When you click any of these tools, the tool options bar offers options unique to the selected tool. To change the selection criteria for the Rectangular Marquee Tool ⬚ and the Elliptical Marquee Tool ◯, click the **Style list arrow** on the tool options bar. Click **Normal** to select the marquee proportions by dragging the ╋. Click **Constrained Aspect Ratio** to set a selection's width-to-height ratio. You can select an area whose width exceeds its height by a factor of two. Click **Fixed Size** to set specific values for the width and height. The three styles are shown in Figure AP-7.

QuickTip

Modify the area selected by ⧉ using the Magnetic Lasso Tool options.

Lasso Tools

The **Lasso Tools** ⬗, ⬙, and ⧉ also appear on the toolbox. To select straight-edged and free-form segments, click the **Lasso Tool** ⬗ or the **Polygonal Lasso Tool** ⬙. Click the **Magnetic Lasso Tool** ⧉ to select an object that has complex edges and is set against a contrasting background. Options for ⬗ and ⬙ include Feather and Anti-aliasing, while the options for ⧉, shown in Figure AP-8, are more extensive.

Magic Wand Tool

Click the **Magic Wand Tool** ⚲ to select an area with a consistent color regardless of the object's complex shape. By adjusting the tolerance, you can control the colors that will be selected.

Selection by color

You can select a specific color or range of colors by using a command on the Select menu. To specify which colors will be selected, click **Select** on the menu bar, then click **Color Range**. When the Color Range dialog box opens, you can use 🖋 to sample colors. By clicking the **Selection option button**, you can view the selection in the preview window, shown in Figure AP-9. Click **OK** when your modifications are complete.

FIGURE AP-7: Styles for Marquee Tools on tool options bar

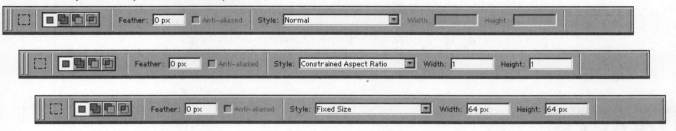

FIGURE AP-8: Magnetic Lasso Tool Options

FIGURE AP-9: Color Range dialog box

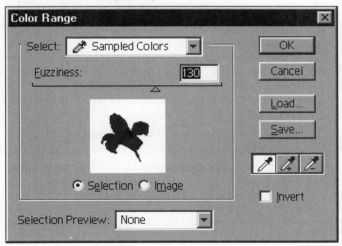

Using Measurement Tools

Successfully working with complex documents requires precise measurements. In Photoshop, you can control the units of measure with which you work. Photoshop also provides tools that make it easier to measure and align objects within a document.

Details

Setting preferences

You can determine the units of measure used in your document. To modify units of measure, click **Edit** on the menu bar, point to **Preferences**, then click **Units & Rulers**. The Preferences dialog box opens. You can adjust the Units & Rulers options, as shown in Figure AP-10. These settings specify the units of measure, the column size settings (width and gutter), and the point/pica size. The width is a column's total horizontal distance, while the gutter is the area of a column in which words are wrapped to the next line. Click **OK** when your modifications are complete.

QuickTip

Rulers are turned on and off independently in Photoshop and ImageReady.

Rulers

To turn on rulers, click **View** on the menu bar, then click **Show Rulers**. To turn off rulers, click **View** on the menu bar, then click **Hide Rulers**. Rulers appear in the units of measure specified in the Units & Rulers Preferences dialog box.

QuickTip

You can create a protractor from an existing line by pressing and holding Alt (Win) or Option (Mac) while dragging to another point on the document.

Measure Tool

Click the **Measure Tool** on the toolbox (hidden underneath the Eyedropper Tool) to calculate the distance between two points in a document. To measure the distance between two points, click on the toolbox, then drag the pointer from one object to another. A measurement line appears, defining the distance you dragged. The line's X (horizontal) and Y (vertical) coordinates appear on the tool options bar, as shown in Figure AP-11. You can delete measurement lines by dragging them out of the document window.

Guides and grids

Guides are non-printing lines that appear in a document and help you align objects. To create a guide, click the **horizontal or vertical ruler** in the document window, then drag a line onto the image. Guides are shown in Figure AP-12. Click the **Move Tool**, place it over a guide, then drag to move an existing guide to a new location. To remove a single guide, drag it out of the document window. To remove all of the guides, click **View** on the menu bar, then click **Clear Guides**. To create a guide *without* displaying rulers, click **View** on the menu bar, then click **New Guide**. Select the type of guide you want (horizontal or vertical) and its position (in pixels), then click **OK**.

A grid is a symmetrical matrix that perfects your layout by aligning objects. To modify grid properties, such as color and spacing, click **Edit** on the menu bar, point to **Preferences**, then click **Guides and Grids**.

FIGURE AP-10: Units & Rulers Preferences dialog box

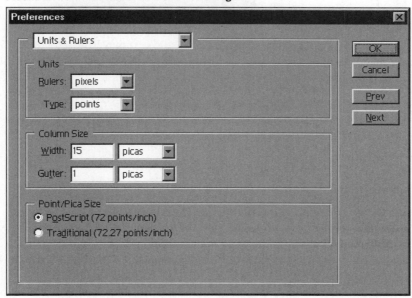

FIGURE AP-11: Tool options bar with Measure Tool selected

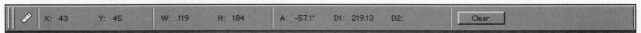

FIGURE AP-12: Guides placed in a document

Photoshop 6.0

Photoshop 6.0

Using Plug-Ins

Although Photoshop offers many powerful and complex features, other programs, called plug-ins, can further extend its capabilities. **Plug-ins** are additional programs—created by Adobe as well as other developers—that expand Photoshop functionality.

QuickTip

Because this page changes frequently, your screen may look different.

Adobe plug-ins

Adobe Photoshop developers created several plug-ins you can use with Photoshop. The plug-ins that accompany Photoshop are added to your computer during installation. Adobe plug-ins import and export files, and automate several processes. Plug-ins work behind the scenes; you have a seamless interface with them. Adobe continually updates its plug-ins (which are located on the Downloads page), as shown in Figure AP-13. The site gives detailed information on available plug-ins, as well as installation instructions.

QuickTip

Adobe continually develops new plug-ins, so check the Photoshop Web site often.

Third-party plug-ins

In addition to Adobe, other manufacturers (called third-party developers) create and market plug-ins for Photoshop. While generally not free, hyperlinks for third-party plug-ins are available on the Photoshop Web site, as shown in Figure AP-14. You can use the hyperlinks to find out more about these plug-ins.

Plug-in preferences

During installation, Photoshop installs plug-ins in a default location on your computer. If you install a third-party plug-in *elsewhere*, you must modify the default location in the Preferences dialog box, otherwise you will not be able to use the new plug-ins. To modify the location of the additional plug-ins, click the **Edit** menu, point to **Preferences**, then click **Plug-Ins & Scratch Disks**. The dialog box shown in Figure AP-15 opens. To change the plug-ins location, click the **Additional Plug-Ins Directory check box**, click the **Choose button**, locate the correct folder on your computer, click **OK**, then click **OK** to close the Preferences dialog box. *You may have to exit the program and restart Photoshop in order for the change to take effect.*

FIGURE AP-13: Adobe Downloads Web page

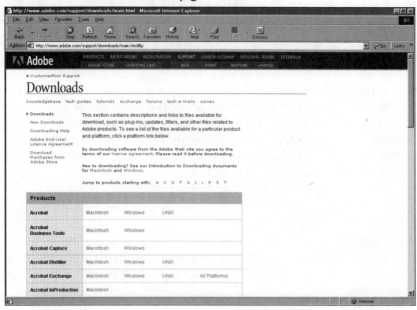

FIGURE AP-14: Adobe Photoshop Third-Party Plug-ins Web page

FIGURE AP-15: Plug-Ins & Scratch Disks Preferences dialog box

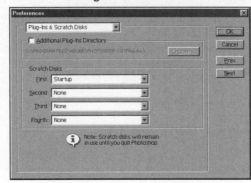

Understanding Print Options

During the course of working with an image, you will want some form of output, such as a hard copy printout. Because the monitor is an RGB device and the printer uses CMYK, even a well-calibrated monitor will never match the colors of your printer. Therefore, printers have standardized color systems, such as Pantone or Toyo. A multi-layer image prints as a **composite image**. In addition to selecting the destination printer, you have many options that influence the output of a document.

Details

QuickTip
The appearance of the Page Setup dialog box and the available options will vary slightly with each printer.

Print options

Before printing a file, you can select your desired print options in the Page Setup dialog box. To open the Page Setup dialog box, shown in Figure AP-16, click **File** on the menu bar, then click **Page Setup**.

The following are descriptions of common printer options in the Page Setup dialog box. Click **OK** when you complete your modifications.

- **Orientation**

  The relationship of the length to the width of the printed page is called **orientation**. A printed page with dimensions 8½" W × 11" L is called **portrait orientation**. A printed page with dimensions 11" W × 8½" L is called **landscape orientation**. To change the orientation, click the **Portrait option button** or **Landscape option button** in the Page Setup dialog box, then click **OK**.

- **Crop marks**

  Pages printed for commercial uses often may need to be trimmed after printing. The trim guidelines are called **crop marks**. These marks can be printed at the corners, center of each edge, or both. Once you open the Page Setup dialog box, click the **Corner Crop Marks check box** and/or **Center Crop Marks check box** to print these marks on your document. Click **OK** to close the Page Setup dialog box.

QuickTip
This background color does not affect the actual document; it is used only in printing.

- **Background**

  You can select a background color that will print on the page, outside the image area. Click the **Background button** in the Page Setup dialog box to change the background color. When you click this button, the Color Picker dialog box opens. Click a **color** in the Color Picker dialog box, click **OK**, then click **OK** in the Page Setup dialog box.

- **Border**

  The border option prints a black border around the image. You can specify the width using inches, points, or millimeters. To add a border to the printed image, click the **Border button** in the Page Setup dialog box. Enter a value in the **Width text box** and select a **unit of measure** using the list arrow in the Border dialog box, then click **OK**. Click **OK** to close the Page Setup dialog box. After you finish with the Page Setup dialog box, you can print by clicking **File** on the menu bar, then clicking **Print**.

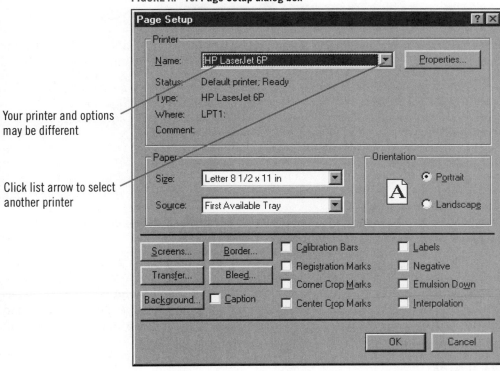

Your printer and options may be different

Click list arrow to select another printer

Choosing a custom color system

Photoshop supports the following color systems: Pantone, Trumatch, HKS, Focoltone, TOYO, ANPA Color, and DIC Color Guide. To choose a supported color system or color library, click the **Set foreground color button** ■ on the toolbox to open the Color Picker dialog box. Click **Custom** in the Color Picker dialog box. The Custom Colors dialog box opens. Click the **Book list arrow**, select a color system, then click **OK**. Figure AP-17 shows the color systems available in the Custom Colors dialog box. The Custom Colors dialog box opens when you click ■. Click the **Default Foreground and Background Colors button** ▣ on the toolbox to return to the default color system.

FIGURE AP-17: Custom Colors dialog box

Photoshop 6.0

Acquiring Images

There are many ways to acquire images for use in Photoshop. In addition to the files that come with the program, you can create your own images in a drawing program, photograph digital images with a digital camera, or scan images using a scanner.

Details

QuickTip

If you did not yet configure your scanner, or have more than one scanner available, you may need to define which scanner will be used. Click File on the menu bar, point to Import, then click an available option.

Scanners

To scan an image directly from Photoshop, click **File** on the menu bar, point to **Import**, then click **TWAIN_32** or a similar option. A dialog box with scanning options opens. Figure AP-18 shows the PaperPort Scan Manager dialog box. Each brand of scanner comes with its own scanning software, so *your screen may look different.* You can use a button in the scanning software to preview the image before it is scanned. You can also change the scanning area using pointers and buttons in the scanning software dialog box.

Digital cameras

Digital cameras capture images just as film cameras do, but they do not use conventional film. Depending on the digital camera you use, the images may be stored on some sort of medium, such as a floppy disk or Smart Card. Similar to scanners, digital cameras have brand-specific imaging software with which you can manipulate and organize the images once you transfer them to your computer. Figure AP-19 shows the Image Expert program window displaying an album.

FIGURE AP-18: PaperPort Scan Manager dialog box

Your scanner dialog box and options may differ

FIGURE AP-19: Image Expert program window

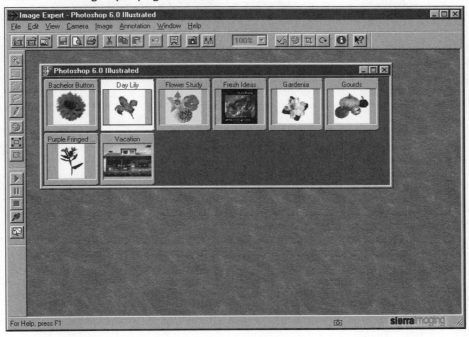

CLUES TO USE

Understanding printer resolution

Commercial artists who use Photoshop want their images to be as crisp and clear as possible. A higher quality image correlates to a higher number of pixels per inch, or **resolution**. Be aware that your output device can be a limiting factor in any high-resolution image. It's easy to spend a lot of time creating a high-resolution image in Photoshop, only to discover that it exceeds your printer's capabilities.

As you increase image resolution, the number of pixels within the image increases in tandem. When you edit an image that has very high resolution, you can make detailed adjustments to ensure that it will reproduce well. Although file size is one indicator of a complex image, an image with low resolution can also be large. In general, a higher resolution setting automatically creates a larger file. **Digital resolution** refers to fineness of output.

Several terms are used to describe resolution. The digital resolution of an image is described in pixels per inch (ppi). Monitor resolution is expressed in ppi. Generally, Windows monitors use a setting of 96 ppi; Macintosh monitors use a setting of 72 ppi. When referring to scanning resolution, this measurement is also expressed as dots per inch (dpi). Lines per inch (lpi) refers to the number of half-tone lines per inch, and has its origin in pre-digital desktop publishing.

Reviewing Keyboard Shortcuts

Sometimes it is easier and faster to use the keyboard than the mouse. You can use key combinations, also called **keyboard shortcuts**, to streamline this process. Some keyboard shortcuts activate tools on the toolbox, others magnify images, and still others engage features in the Layers palette. Table AP-1 lists commonly used keyboard shortcuts that activate toolbox tools. Table AP-2 lists shortcuts that help navigate palettes, and Table AP-3 lists shortcuts for tools in the Extract dialog box.

TABLE AP-1: Keyboard shortcuts

activate tool	by pressing	activate tool	by pressing
	M		V
	L		W
	J		B
	S		Y
	E		N
	R		O
	P		T
	U		G
	K		I
	H		Z
	D		X
	Q		F

TABLE AP-2: Palette shortcuts

palette	task	by pressing
All	Show/Hide palette	[Tab]
Layers	Show/Hide palette	[F7]
Layers	Move down stack	[Alt][[ ]
Layers	Move up stack	[Alt][ ]]
Brushes	Show/Hide palette	[F5]
Info	Show/Hide palette	[F8]
Actions	Show/Hide palette	[F9]

TABLE AP-3: Extract Image shortcuts

activate tool	by pressing	activate tool	by pressing
	B		I
	G		Z
	E		H

Glossary

Action A series of tasks that you record and save to play back later as a single command using buttons in the Actions palette.

Active layer The layer highlighted in the Layers palette that appears in parenthesis in the document window title bar.

Additive colors When combined, the colors create white. When the values of R, G, and B are zero, the result is black; when the values are all 255, white results.

Adjustment layer An additional layer for which you can specify eleven specific color adjustments. The adjustment layer acts as a screen, allowing underlying layer objects to appear.

Adobe ImageReady An integral part of Photoshop used to create buttons, rollovers, and animations.

Alpha channel Specific color information added to a default channel.

Ambience property Controls the balance between the light source and the overall light in an image.

Animation The phenomenon of moving images, created by placing images in the same location, and adjusting the timing between their appearances.

Animation delays The length of time one frame appears before the animation advances to the next frame.

Anti-aliasing Partially fills in pixel edges, resulting in smooth-edge type and is recommended for large type. This feature lets your type maintain its crisp appearance.

Artistic filters Replicates natural or traditional media effects.

Auto-slice A slice created automatically by ImageReady.

Background color Used to make gradient fills and fill in areas of an image that have been erased. The default background color is white.

Background Eraser Tool Lets you selectively remove pixels from a document, just as you would use a pencil eraser to remove unwanted written marks. The erased areas become transparent.

Base color The original color of the image.

Base layer The bottom layer in a clipping group, which serves as the group's mask.

Baseline An invisible line on which type rests.

Baseline shift The distance type appears from its original position.

Bitmap A geometric arrangement of different color dots on a rectangular grid.

Bitmap mode Uses black or white color values to represent image pixels. A good choice for images with subtle color gradations, such as photographs or painted images.

Bitmap type Type that is composed of pixels and may develop jagged edges when enlarged.

Blend color The color that is applied to the base color when a blending mode is applied to a layer.

Blending modes Sixteen possible ways to manipulate the appearance of a layer's base color using painting and editing tools.

Blur filters Used to soften a selection or image.

Brightness The measurement of relative lightness or darkness of a color (measured as a percentage from 0% [black] to 100% [white]).

Brush Strokes filters Mimics fine arts effects such as a brush and ink stroke.

Channels Used to store information about the color elements contained in each channel.

Photoshop 6.0 | Glossary

Channels palette Lists all channel information. The top channel is a composite channel—a combination of all the default channels. You can hide channels in the same manner as you hide layers, by clicking the eye button.

Character palette Helps you control type properties. The Character palette is located on the tool options bar.

Clipping group Links contiguous layers.

CMYK image Has at least four channels (one each for cyan, magenta, yellow, and black).

Color channel An area where color information is stored. Every Photoshop image has at least one channel and can have a maximum of twenty-four color channels.

Color mode Used to determine how to display and print an image. Each mode is based on established models used in color reproduction.

Color Picker Feature that lets you choose a color from a color spectrum.

Color separation Result of converting an RGB image into a CMYK image.

Composite channel The top channel in the Channels palette that is a combination of all the default channels.

Contact sheet Compilation of thirty thumbnail images (per sheet) from a specific folder.

Crisp Anti-aliasing setting that gives type more definition and makes it appear sharper.

Crop Exclude part of an image. Cropping hides areas of an image without losing resolution quality.

Crop marks Page notations where trimming will occur can be printed at the corners, center of each edge, or both.

Darken Only option Replaces light pixels with darker pixels.

Default channels The color channels automatically contained in a document.

Diffuse filter Makes layer contents look less focused.

Digimarc filters Embed a digital watermark that stores copyright information into an image.

Digital camera Camera that captures images on electronic media rather than film. Its images are in a standard digital format and can be downloaded for computer use.

Distort filters Used to create three-dimensional or other reshaping effects. Some of the types of distortions you can produce include Glass, Pinch, Ripple, Shear, Spherize, Twirl, Wave, and Zigzag.

Dithering Occurs when a Web browser attempts to display colors that are not included in its native color palette.

Drop shadow This effect adds what looks like a colored layer of identical text behind the selected type. The default shadow color is black.

Exposure property Lighten or darken the lighting effects ellipse.

Extract feature Used to isolate a foreground object from its background.

Filters Alters the look of an image and gives it a special, customized appearance by applying special effects, such as distortions, changes in lighting, and blurring.

Flattening Merges all visible layers into one layer, which is named the Background layer. Greatly reduces the size of your document by merging all the visible layers and deletes all of the hidden layers.

Font family Represents a complete set of characters, letters, and symbols for a particular typeface. Font families are generally divided into three categories: serif, sans serif, and symbol.

Foreground color Used to paint, fill, and stroke selections. The default foreground color is black.

Gamut The range of displayed colors in a color model.

Gloss property Controls the amount of surface reflectance on the lighted surfaces.

Gradient fill   Used to make colors appear to blend into one another. A gradient's appearance is determined by its beginning and ending points. Photoshop contains five gradient fill tools.

Grayscale image   Can contain up to 256 shades of gray. Pixels can have brightness values from 0 (black) to 255 (white).

Grayscale mode   Uses up to 256 shades of gray, assigning a brightness value from 0 (black) to 255 (white) to each pixel.

Guides   Horizontal and vertical lines that you create to help you align objects. Guide lines display in light blue.

Handles   Small boxes that appear along the perimeter of a selection and are used to change the size of an image.

History palette   Contains a record of each action performed during a Photoshop session. Up to twenty levels of Undo are available through the History palette.

Hotspot   Area within an object that is assigned a URL.

Hue   The color reflected from/transmitted through an object and expressed as a degree (between 0° and 360°). Each hue is identified by a color name such as red or green.

Image map   Composed of multiple hotspots and can be circular, rectangular, or a polygon.

Kerning   The amount of space between two characters.

Keyboard shortcuts   Combinations of keys that can be used to work faster and more efficiently.

Landscape orientation   A document with the long edge of the paper at the top and bottom.

Layer mask   Can cover an entire layer or specific areas within a layer. When a layer contains a mask, an additional thumbnail displays in the Layer palette.

Layers   Unique to Photoshop, objects are stored in individual areas. The advantage is that individual effects can be isolated and manipulated without affecting the rest of the image. The disadvantage is that layers can increase the size of your file.

Layers palette   Displays all the layers within an active document. You can use the Layers palette to create, delete, merge, copy, or reposition layers.

Leading   The vertical amount of space between lines of type.

Lighten Only option   Replaces dark pixels with light pixels.

Lighting Effects filter   Applies lighting effects to an image.

Lossless   A file compression format in which no data is discarded.

Lossy format   File format that discards data during the compression process.

Lossy GIF format   Compresses files while maintaining image quality.

Luminosity   The remaining light and dark values that result when a color image is converted to grayscale.

Magic Eraser Tool   Lets you erase areas in an image that have similar colored pixels.

Marquee   A broken line that surrounds an area and can be edited or dragged into another document.

Material property   Controls parts of an image that reflect the light source color.

Menu bar   Contains menus from which you can choose Photoshop commands.

Merging layers   Process of combining multiple image layers into one layer.

Mode   Amount of color data that can be stored in a given file format. Also determines the color model used to display and print a document.

Model   Determines how pigments combine to produce resulting colors and is determined by the color mode.

Monitor calibration   Process that displays printed colors accurately on your monitor.

Monotype spacing   Spacing in which each character occupies the same amount of space.

Motion Blur filter Adjusts the angle of the blur, as well as the distance the blur appears to travel.

Noise filters Add or remove pixels with randomly distributed color levels.

Normal blend mode The default blending mode.

Opacity Determines the percentage of transparency. A layer with 100% opacity will obstruct objects in the layers beneath it, while a layer with 1% opacity will appear nearly transparent.

Optimized image Reduce an image size without sacrificing image quality.

Orientation Direction an image appears on the page—portrait or landscape.

Other filters Allows you to create your own filters, modify masks, or make quick color adjustments.

Outline type Type that is mathematically defined and can be scaled to any size without losing the smooth appearance of its edges.

Out-of gamut indicator Indicates that the current color falls beyond the accurate print or display range.

Palettes Floating windows that can be moved and are used to modify objects. Palettes containing tabs can be separated and moved to another group. Each palette contains a menu that can be viewed by clicking the list arrow in its upper-right corner.

Picture package Contains multiple sizes of a single document selected from eleven layouts.

Pixel Each dot in a bitmapped image that represents a color or shade.

Pixelate filters Used to sharply define a selection.

Plug-ins Additional programs, created by Adobe and other developers, that expand Photoshop's functionality.

Points Unit of measure for font sizes. Traditionally, 1 inch is equivalent to 72.27 points. The default Photoshop type size is 12 points.

Portrait orientation A document with the short edge of the paper at the top and bottom.

PostScript A programming language, created by Adobe, that optimized printed text and graphics.

Preferences Used to control the Photoshop environment using your specifications.

Properties color swatch Changes the ambient light around the lighting spotlight.

Proportional spacing Spacing in which each character takes up a different amount of space, depending on its width.

Radial Blur filter Adjusts the amount of blur and the blur method (Spin or Zoom).

Rasterize Converts a type layer to an image layer.

Render filters Transform three-dimensional shapes and simulated light reflections in an image.

Resolution Number of pixels per inch.

Result color The outcome of the blend color applied to the base color.

RGB image Has three channels—one each for red, green, and blue.

Rollover Changes an object's appearance when the pointer passes over (or clicks) a specific area of the image.

Rulers Rulers can help you precisely measure and position an object, but are not shown by default. Rulers can be displayed using the View menu.

Sans serif fonts Fonts that do not have tails or strokes at the end of some characters and are commonly used in headlines.

Saturation The strength or purity of the color, representing the amount of gray in proportion to hue. Saturation is measured as a percentage from 0% (gray), to 100% (fully saturated). Also known as *chroma*.

Save As Command that lets you create a copy of the open document, using a new name.

Scanner Electronic device that converts print material into an electronic file.

Selection An area in an image that is surrounded by a selection marquee.

Serif fonts Fonts that have a tail, or stroke, at the end of some characters. These tails make it easier for the eye to recognize words; therefore, serif fonts are generally used in text passages.

Sharpen More filter Increases the contrast of adjacent pixels and can focus blurry images.

Sketch filters Apply a texture or create a hand-drawn effect.

Slices Smaller sections of an image used to create unique effects. When a file is opened for the first time in ImageReady, the entire document is contained in a single slice. When you create a slice, ImageReady automatically renumbers existing slices.

Smart Blur filter Adjusts the quality, radius, and threshold of the blur.

Snapshot A temporary copy of an image that contains the history states made up to that point. You can create multiple snapshots in an image and you can switch between snapshots.

State Individual thumbnails in the Rollover palette or individual entries in the History palette.

Status bar This area is located at the bottom of the program window (Win) or the bottom of the document window (Mac) and displays information such as the file size of the active window and a description of the active tool.

Stroking the edges The process of making a selection or layer stand out by surrounding it with a border.

Style Eighteen pre-designed styles that can be applied to buttons.

Stylize filters Produce a painted or impressionistic effect.

Subtractive colors The result of cyan, magenta, and yellow absorbing all color and producing black.

Swatches palette Contains available colors that can be selected for use as a foreground or background color. You can also add your own colors to the Swatches palette.

Symbol fonts Used to display unique characters (such as $, ÷, or ™).

Table Rectangular object made up of columns and rows and used for storing data.

Texture filters Give the appearance of depth or substance.

This Layer slider Used to specify the range of pixels that will be blended on the active layer.

Threshold The Normal mode when working with bitmapped images. The threshold is the starting point for applying other blending modes.

Thumbnail Contains a miniature picture of the layer's content, appears to the left of the layer name, and may be turned on or off.

Title bar Displays the program name and filename of the open document. The title bar also contains a control menu box, a Close button, and resizing buttons.

Tolerance The range of pixels that will be considered, and opacity, you can determine which pixels will be selected. The lower the tolerance, the closer the color is to the selection.

Tool options bar Displays the settings for the currently active tool. The tool options bar is located directly under the menu bar, but can be moved anywhere in the work area for easier access.

Toolbox Contains tools for frequently used commands. On the face of a tool is a graphic representation of its function. Place the pointer over each button to display a ScreenTip, which tells you the name or function of that button.

Tracking The insertion of a uniform amount of space between characters.

Tweening The process of selecting multiple frames, then inserting transitional frames between them. This effect makes frames appear to blend into one another and gives the animation a more fluid appearance.

Photoshop 6.0

Twirl filter   Applies a circular effect to a layer.

Type   A layer containing text. Each character is measured in points. In PostScript measurement, 1 inch is equivalent to 72 points. In traditional measurement, 1 inch is equivalent to 72.27 points.

Underlying Layer slider   Used to specify the range of pixels that will be blended on lower visible layers.

URL   Uniform Resource Locator. Formal name for a Web address.

User-slice   A slice you create in ImageReady.

Video filters   Restricts colors to those acceptable for television reproduction and smooth video images.

Warp Text   Feature that lets you add dimension and style to type.

Web image gallery   Contains a thumbnail index page of all exported images, the actual JPEG images, and any included links.

Web-safe colors   216 colors that display on the Web without dithering.

Wind filter   Conveys the feeling of direction and motion on the layer to which it is applied.

Work area   The entire window: from the menu bar at the top of the window, to the status bar at the bottom border of the program window.

Index

Index

Index

Index

resolution-dependent, 26
resolution of printers, 207
restoring default settings, 196
result color, 98
RGB images channels, 38
RGB model, 26
Ripple filter, 62
Rollover palette, 178, 180
rollovers, 170
rulers, 6, 200
  showing, 52
  units of measure, 28

▶ S

Sandstone texture, 62
sans serif fonts, 50–51
saturation, 26
Save As dialog box, 8, 88
Save For Web dialog box, 172
Save Optimized As dialog box, 172
saving
  documents, 8
  files, 12, 196
  files for Web, 181
scanners, 2, 15, 206
Scratches filter, 122
scratches or stains, 152
Screen mode, 98
.SCT (ScitexCT) file format, 3
selecting objects, 198
selection box color, 198
selections, 80
  applying filter, 124
  borders, 156
  feathering, 100
  masks hiding, 100
  snapping to edge of object, 156
  specific, 156
selection tools, 81
Selective Color adjustment layers, 110–111
serif fonts, 50–51
Sharp anti-aliasing, 58
Sharpen filter, 122
Sharpen More filter, 38, 122
Shear filter, 62, 122
shortcut keys, 6
Show/Hide layer button, 12
single-sheet feed scanners, 15
Sketch filters, 122

slices, 170, 176
Slice Select Tool, 176, 178, 180
Slice Tool, 176
Smart Blur filter, 124
SmartMedia card, 15
Snap feature, 32
snapshots, 158
Soft Light blend mode, 98
Solarize filter, 122
Spatter filter, 122
special effects, 62
specific selections, 156
Spherize filter, 62
Sponge filter, 122
stacking layers, 86
Stained Glass filter, 122
Stamp filter, 122
states, 158
status bar, 6
Stroke dialog box, 32
stroking the edges, 32
strong anti-aliasing, 58
Style dialog box, 60
Style Options dialog box, 175
styles, 175
Styles palette, 175
Stylize filters, 62, 122, 128
subtractive colors, 26
Swatches palette, 28, 30, 55
switching between snapshots, 158
symbol fonts, 50

▶ T

tables, 176
tasks, undoing and redoing, 2
temporary storage file, 160
text, 2, 49
  See also type
  distortions, 62
  fundamentals, 50
  moving, 52
  special effects, 62
Texture filters, 122, 136
textures, 136
Texturizer filter, 62
.TGA or .VDA (Targa) file format, 3
third-party plug-ins, 202
This Layer sliders, 106
threshold, 98

Index